LEGAL ISSUES JOURNAL
Volume 10, Issue 1

December 2024

The UK Law and Society Association

LEGAL ISSUES JOURNAL
Volume 10, Issue 1
December 2024

Legal Issues Journal (LIJ) is a multidisciplinary, peer-reviewed, nonprofit journal providing a platform for the dissemination of cross-disciplinary research to enable novel solutions to societal questions. We welcome original research and other scholarly works which address such questions by bringing together two or more disciplines, across fields such as psychology, law, genetics, sociology and philosophy. Of particular interest are topics focusing on justice, equality, education, human behaviour, decision making, societal structures, and ethics. LIJ is fully independent, providing the certainty of quality-based evaluation.

ISBNs
9798303549128
9798230644217

Published by Sulis Academic Press
An Imprint of Sulis International
Los Angeles | Dallas | London
www.sulisinternational.com

Table of Contents

Legal Issues Journal 10(1) 2024: 1–7. ©The UK Law and Society Association

Opinion: Sleep and the Law

Alice M. Gregory,[1] Juan J Madrid-Valero,[2] Ciara Bird[3]

In this piece, we flag the importance of sleep for human behaviour. Sleep is essential for human functioning yet historically has been relatively neglected in various areas of psychological research such as that focusing on psychopathology (e.g., Gregory & Sadeh, 2016). Here we note empirical data and legal cases and considerations which emphasise the potential importance of further considering sleep in the context of the legal system. We argue for the need to conduct additional high-quality systematic research in this area, as well as the importance of interdisciplinary collaborations to contribute to a more comprehensive understanding of human behaviour within the legal system and to maximise the impact of this work.

Sleep has many functions including supporting emotional regulation (Palmer & Alfano, 2017) as well as memory and cognition (Girardeau & Lopes-Dos-Santos, 2021). Consequentially, missing out on sleep can result in poorer emotional regulation as well as have a negative impact on cognitive functions including attention and decision-making. It follows that sleep deprivation could play a

[1]Department of Psychology, Goldsmiths, University of London, London, United Kingdom. Corresponding author: a.gregory@gold.ac.uk.
[2]Department of Human Anatomy and Psychobiology, Faculty of Psychology, University of Murcia, Murcia, Spain.
[3]LLB (Hons), Barrister at Law, MSc UCL (Dist) - UCL, Registered Psychotherapist (UKCP) and Counselling Psychologist in training (DCPsych).

role in certain crimes, including those committed in the context of emotional outbursts ('provocation') or due to significant failures (e.g., falling asleep at the wheel or making serious errors at work).

Sleep quality and disorders also need to be considered in this context, with untreated or undisclosed narcolepsy or sleep apnea examples of disorders which could lead to falling asleep with serious consequences and legal ramifications, potentially adding a new dimension to legal proceedings. Indeed, undiagnosed severe sleep apnea was flagged as a possible contributor to the high-profile Long Island Rail Road Collision in 2017 in which 108 people were injured (NTSB, 2017). More generally, untreated sleep apnea is a risk factor for other outcomes, such as car accidents (Tregear et al., 2009).

Such findings highlight the legal obligations of those with certain sleep disorders. While patients may legally be able to refuse treatment for a sleep disorder, they do not have a right to ignore risks to others caused by this decision (see Brown, 2022). The employer also holds legal obligations linked to their employees' sleep – and may hold vicarious liability for sleep-related accidents occurring during work hours. In industries where safety is paramount (e.g., for doctors, pilots etc.) there may also be regulation restricting work hours and reducing tiredness (Brown, 2022). Where a sleep disorder qualifies as a disability this will have implications for reasonable adjustments required by law. Working conditions (e.g., shift work) which are deemed to cause harm (e.g., cancer) may result in compensation claims (Erren et al., 2009).

Beyond employment law, early school start times, often considered to be out of sync with the internal timing of young people with consequential implications for accidents and missed potential, could hold implications for education law. What is more, if sleep is considered a fundamental human right, legal implications for housing, homelessness and detention could follow. Governments and local authorities might also want to consider promoting sleep quality via policies and public campaigns.

As well as potential legal implications of the sleep disorders narcolepsy and sleep apnea, other sleep disorders have also been flagged in the legal context. These include sexomnia, which involves sexual behaviours related to sleep and may occur during a confusional arousal or in the context of sleep-walking (American Academy of Sleep Medicine, 2023). This sleep disorder has led to sexual assaults (Dubessy et al., 2017) and been presented as a defence against allegations of rape with a recent case being dismissed because it was deemed possible that the alleged victim could have experienced an episode of sexomnia, something she strongly contested (Ailes, 2022). Sleep-walking and confusional arousals have also been considered in defence against accusations of violent crimes (Ebrahim & Fenwick, 2008; Ingravallo et al., 2014).

In addition to the relevance of sleep-related variables to crimes committed and the potential defence (which could potentially be used to argue diminished capacity, lack of intent or involuntary behaviour), the sleep of others involved in the legal system may be worthy of further consideration. Given associations between sleep and memory, the quality and accuracy of an eyewitness testimony may vary as a function of the way a witness has slept prior to the event on which they are reporting; or whether statements are taken before or after periods of sleep. Some data support a role for sleep, and one report found that self-reported sleep quality prior to witnessing a mock crime, predicted the accuracy for which certain details were reported (Carlson et al., 2023). This chimes well with previous work showing that poorer self-reported sleep quality and greater sleepiness were associated with poorer accuracy in reporting the peripheral details of a crime (Thorley, 2013). Other reports have examined the role of sleep deprivation for false memories, finding that the former could increase the latter under certain conditions but not others (Frenda et al., 2014). Null findings have also been reported, and one study found no support for the idea that sleeping after witnessing a crime and before assessing a line-up improved eyewitness identification (Morgan et al., 2019). These mixed results for different sleep variables suggest that further empirical study, systematic reviews and meta-analyses may help to establish the full significance, magnitude, and the way in which sleep could be relevant to eyewitness testimony.

Decision-making within the legal context may also be impacted significantly by sleep/circadian factors. One striking report found that judges in the US handed out sentences on the Monday following the shift to daylight savings (which is often accompanied by missing out on sleep) that were 5% longer when compared to other Mondays (Cho et al., 2017). It is however noteworthy that a further consideration of these data suggested that modelling decisions impacted these results and that therefore this effect (if it exists) may be smaller than first considered (Spamann, 2018).

While the full extent of the importance of sleep for different aspects of the legal system is currently unclear, research and reports to date suggests that it might be fruitful to further consider this line of enquiry. It is beyond the aims of the authors (who have written this piece in our roles as sleep researchers and psychologists) to make suggestions about the way in which this information (if found to be robust) should be incorporated into legal recommendations and considerations – and it is and only with interdisciplinary collaborative research and discussion that this will become clearer. At the very least, further research should be conducted to examine robust effect sizes and legal experts should be aware of the role of sleep on human behaviour per se to decide if and how this needs to be further considered in a legal context.

Conflicts of interests

Alice Gregory is an advisor for a project initially sponsored by Johnson's Baby. She is a consultant for Perrigo (2021+). She receives royalties for two books, **Nodding Off** (Bloomsbury Sigma, 2018) and **The Sleepy Pebble** (Flying Eye, 2019) and a sleep gift (**The Gift of Sleep,** Lawrence King Publishers, 2023). She was previously a CEO of **Sleep Universal LTD** (2022). She is a regular contributor to **BBC Focus Magazine** and has contributed to other outlets (such as **The Conversation, The Guardian** and **Balance Magazine**). She occasionally receives sample products related to sleep (e.g., blue light blocking glasses) and has given a paid talk to a business (**Investec**). She is a specialist subject editor at **JCPP** (sleep) for which she receives a small honorarium. She has contributed a paid article to **Neurodiem**.

References

Ailes, E. (2022). Claims I had sexsomnia destroyed my rape case. BBC. Retrieved 19-1-2024 from https://www.bbc.com/news/uk-63116989.

American Academy of Sleep Medicine. (2023). International Classification of Sleep Disorders (3rd text revision ed.). American Academy of Sleep Medicine.

Brown, D. B. (2022). Legal obligations of persons who have sleep disorders or who treat or hire them In M. H. Kryger, T. Roth, & C. A. Goldstein (Eds.), Priciples and Practice of Sleep Medicine (7th ed.). Elsevier.

Carlson, M., Carlson, C., & Fitzsimmons, C. (2023). The sleepy eyewitness: Self-reported sleep predicts eyewitness memory. J App Res Mem and Cog, 12(4), 513-530.

Cho, K., Barnes, C. M., & Guanara, C. L. (2017). Sleepy Punishers Are Harsh Punishers. Psychol Sci, 28(2), 242-247. https://doi.org/10.1177/0956797616678437

Dubessy, A. L., Leu-Semenescu, S., Attali, V., Maranci, J. B., & Arnulf, I. (2017). Sexsomnia: A Specialized Non-REM Parasomnia? Sleep, 40(2). https://doi.org/10.1093/sleep/zsw043

Ebrahim, I. O., & Fenwick, P. (2008). Sleep-related automatism and the law. Med Sci Law, 48(2), 124-136. https://doi.org/10.1258/rsmmsl.48.2.124

Legal Issues Journal 10(1) 2024: 1–7. ©The UK Law and Society Association

Erren, T. C., Falaturi, P., Morfeld, P., & Reiter, R. J. (2009). Shift work and cancer: risk, compensation, challenges. BMJ, 339, b3430. https://doi.org/10.1136/bmj.b3430

Frenda, S. J., Patihis, L., Loftus, E. F., Lewis, H. C., & Fenn, K. M. (2014). Sleep deprivation and false memories. Psychol Sci, 25(9), 1674-1681. https://doi.org/10.1177/0956797614534694

Girardeau, G., & Lopes-Dos-Santos, V. (2021). Brain neural patterns and the memory function of sleep. Science, 374(6567), 560-564. https://doi.org/10.1126/science.abi8370

Gregory, A. M., & Sadeh, A. (2016). Annual Research Review: Sleep problems in childhood psychiatric disorders--a review of the latest science. J Child Psychol Psychiatry, 57(3), 296-317. https://doi.org/10.1111/jcpp.12469

Ingravallo, F., Poli, F., Gilmore, E. V., Pizza, F., Vignatelli, L., Schenck, C. H., & Plazzi, G. (2014). Sleep-related violence and sexual behavior in sleep: a systematic review of medical-legal case reports. J Clin Sleep Med, 10(8), 927-935. https://doi.org/10.5664/jcsm.3976

Morgan, D. P., Tamminen, J., Seale-Carlisle, T. M., & Mickes, L. (2019). The impact of sleep on eyewitness identifications. R Soc Open Sci, 6(12), 170501. https://doi.org/10.1098/rsos.170501

NTSB. (2017). Derailment of Long Island Railroad passenger train in Brooklyn, NY. Retrieved 19-1-2024 from https://www.ntsb.gov/investigations/Pages/DCA17FR002.aspx.

Palmer, C. A., & Alfano, C. A. (2017). Sleep and emotion regulation: An organizing, integrative review. Sleep Med Rev, 31, 6-16. https://doi.org/10.1016/j.smrv.2015.12.006

Spamann, H. (2018). Are Sleepy Punishers Really Harsh Punishers? Comment on Cho, Barnes, and Guanara (2017). Psychol Sci, 29(6), 1006-1009. https://doi.org/10.1177/0956797617720239

Thorley, C. (2013). The Effects of Recent Sleep Duration, Sleep Quality, and Current Sleepiness on Eyewitness Memory [Article]. Applied Cognitive Psychology, 27(5), 690-695. https://doi.org/10.1002/acp.2938

Tregear, S., Reston, J., Schoelles, K., & Phillips, B. (2009). Obstructive sleep apnea and risk of motor vehicle crash: systematic review and meta-analysis. J Clin Sleep Med, 5(6), 573-581.

Legal Issues Journal 10(1) 2024: 9–82. ©The UK Law and Society Association

Differences between CISG and ULIS

Dr Bashayer Al-Mukhaizeem[1]

This research facilitates the discovery of the relative strengths and weakness of CISG and ULIS and enhances wider and deeper comprehensibility of how and where CISG's Articles conflict with ULIS. Notwithstanding, this study involves looking back and draws a distinction between the past and present on the grounds that ULIS itself is regarded as a historical factor in the development of CISG. In clarifying the debate, it is important to synthesise the differences between ULIS's and CISG's provisions, which calls for a contextual approach, with an analytical eye, to appraise both Conventions. A comparability study provides a deeply informed perspective with which to achieve a better understanding of the practical and doctrinal purposes of the two legal systems, namely by asking how CISG and ULIS tackle similar contentions with different techniques. Comparison is considered as an effective experiment to improve and reform current practices.

[1]Kuwait International Law School. Corresponding author: b.al-mukhaizeem@kilaw.edu.kw.

Legal Issues Journal 10(1) 2024: 9–82. ©The UK Law and Society Association

Introduction

Universal commerce has increased sharply since 1955[2] due to the integration of world markets and the dissolution of barriers to the flow of goods,[3] enabling businesses to reach the rest of the world faster than ever before.[4] Global trade has grown because of the limited natural resources of individual states which makes the notion of self-sufficiency implausible.[5] International sales account for two-thirds of world trade.[6] The proponents of international trade assert its necessity for many reasons. First, it helps nations to attain economic prosperity[7] and higher living standards. International sales make Mitsubishi Company, for instance, wealthier than the economies of Denmark, Turkey and Thailand.[8] Second, it exploits productive ability,[9] which fosters the alleviation of poverty.[10] Finally, it fosters better understanding between nations.[11]

Due to the large-scale movement of goods throughout the world, the need for an international convention to govern international transactions has become crucial to secure a healthy and reliable

---

[2] Ray August, International Business Law: Texts, Cases and Readings (London, Prentice Hall 2000) 354.

[3] Joseph Stiglitz, Globalization and its Discontents (London, Penguin Books 2002) 9.

[4] Peter Van den Bossche; Werner Zdouc cited Firedman, The Law and Policy of the World Trade Organization (Cambridge University Press 2014) 5.

[5] Frederick van der Ploeg, 'Natural Resources: Curse or Blessing?' (2011) 49(2) Journal of Economic Literature, 399.

[6] Michael Woodin; Caroline Lucas, Green Alternatives to Globalisation (London, Pluto Press 2004) 18.

[7] Stiglitz (n 2) 4; Bossche; Zdouc (n 3) 6.

[8] Woodin; Lucas (n 5) 18.

[9] ibid 20.

[10] Stiglitz (n 2) 5.

[11] Bossche; Zdouc (n 3) 16-17 & 21.

from of globalisation.[12] International conventions seek to achieve equity between the contracting parties, and solve their disputes outside of the realms of domestic law,[13] which is neither compatible with global trading[14] nor predictable.[15] International conventions seek to accomplish the goal of harmonising the differences[16] between national laws and provide the parties with knowledge of the rules which govern their contract in advance.[17] Fairness and neutrality, which is desired by trading businesses, can be reached by using a supranational instrument[18] as opposed to partial national law,[19] which would be more familiar and beneficial to one party

[12]ibid cited Coase, 31. Globalisation is not a new phenomenon but it existed even before the First World War. There were large overseas flows of commodities and investments. ibid 6.

[13]Giuditta Cordero-Moss, International Commercial Contract (Cambridge University Press 2014) 70.

[14]Roy Goode; Herbert Kronke; Ewan McKendrick, Transnational Commercial Law (Oxford University Press 2011) 52; Michael Bonell, 'The UNIDROIT Principles of International Commercial Contracts and the Harmonisation of International Sales Law' (2002) 36 Revue Juridique Themis, 286.

[15]Jan Dalhuisen, Dalhuisen on Transnational Comparative, Commercial, Financial and Trade Law Volume 3: Financial Products, Financial Services and Financial Regulation (Oxford, Hart Publishing 2013) 627-629. Bossche; Zdouc (n 3) 32.

[16]James Fawcett; Jonathan Harris; Michael Bridge, International Sale of Goods in the Conflict of Laws (Oxford University Press 2012) 937; Shani Salama, 'Pragmatic Responses to Interpretive Impediments: Article 7 of the CISG, an Inter-American Application' (2007) 38 The University of Miami Inter-American Law Review, 243.

[17]Salama (n 15) 227; C. Bianca, Michael Bonell, Commentary on the International Sales Law: The 1980 Vienna Sales Convention (Milan, Giuffre 1987) 66.

[18]Ewan Mckendrick, Contract Law (Palgrave Macmillan 2013) [9].

[19]Herbert Kronke, 'The UN Sales Convention, the UNIDROIT Contract Principles and the Way Beyond' (2205) 25 The Journal of Law and Commerce 462; Ulrich Magnus, 'Interpretation and Gap-filling in the CISG and in the CESL' (2012) 11(3) Journal of International Trade Law & Policy 266-267.

than the other.[20] Some domestic laws align with the seller while others are buyer-friendly,[21] and other municipal laws are biased towards their nations. Domestic law may therefore disturb the equilibrium of the contract, which is a critical principle of impartiality.[22] Thus, international conventions encourage fair and effective cross-border contracts for commercial activities,[23] promoting interdependent relationships.[24] Attempts to establish such conventions began in the 1920s with the International Institute for Unification of Private Law (UNIDROIT), which sought to harmonise the law among various jurisdictions[25] associated with the international sale of goods.[26] The Uniform Law for the International Sale of Goods (ULIS)[27] was completed in 1964 but failed to achieve international agreement on principles for the sale of

---

[20]Alejandro Garro, 'The Gap-filling Role of The UNIDROIT Principles in International Sales Law: Some Comments on the Interplay between the Principles and the CISG' (1995) 69 Tulane Law Review, 1153-1159; Michael Bonell, An International Restatement of Contract Law: The UNIDROIT Principles of International Commercial Contracts (New York, Transnational Publishers 2004) 307.

[21]Goode et al cited Anderson (n 13) 276.

[22]For example, CISG Art. 74. Using a supranational instrument facilitates predictability and regulates the incorporation of national financial systems into one borderless global economy. Bossche; Zdouc (n 3) 6; Magnus (n 18) 267.

[23]Bossche; Zdouc cited Jackson (n 3) 32.

[24]ibid 32.

[25]Magnus (n 18) 267.

[26]Jason Chuah, Law of International Trade: Cross-border Commercial Transactions (London, Thomson Reuters 2013) 175; Esin Örücü; David Nelken, Comparative Law (Oxford, Hart Publishing 2007) 264-277.

[27]It is also called the Hague Convention 1964.

goods[28] (receiving only nine ratifications)[29] on the grounds that it was a purely European project drafted without the participation of developing countries.[30] Furthermore, ULIS emerged during the era of decolonisation which made many developing countries reluctant to enter into international conventions as they were focusing on developing their own economic and political structures.[31] In 1980, the UN Commission on International Trade Law (UNCITRAL) created, with input from more than 60 countries,[32] the UN Convention on Contracts for International Sale of Goods (CISG),[33] which

---

[28]John Honnold, 'The Uniform Law for the International Sale of Goods: The Hague Convention of 1964' (1964)13(3) The American Journal of Comparative Law 394; August (n 1) 535.

[29]Sonia Viejobueno, 'Progress through Compromise: the 1980 United Nations Convention on Contracts for the International Sale of Goods' (1995) 28 (2) The Comparative and International Law Journal of Southern Africa 201; Chuah (n 25) 175; August (n 1) 535.

[30]Goode et al (n 13) 257; August (n 1) 535; Gyula Eörsi, 'A propos the 1980 Vienna Convention on Contracts for the International Sale of Goods' (1983) 31(2) The American Journal of Comparative Law, 335.

[31]M. Shafiq, M, The UN Convention on the International Sale of Goods (Cairo, Dar Alnahda Alarabeya 1998) 25; Leon Trakman; Nicola Ranieri, Regionalism in International Investment Law (Oxford University Press 2013) 479. Also, some countries found that ULIS' substantive legal content was not convincing. Goode et al (n 13) 257; Arthur Rosett, 'Critical Reflections on the United Nations Convention on Contracts for the International Sale of Goods' (1984) 45 Ohio State Law Journal 269. ULIS is still applied in a few countries such as Gambia. San Marino withdrew from ULIS in 1st March 2013 and ratified CISG which came into force on 1st March 2013. UNIDROIT, 'Status - Convention Relating to a Uniform Law on The International Sale of Goods (ULIS) (The Hague, 1964)' <https://www.unidroit.org/instruments/international-sales/ulis-1964/status/> [accessed 8/10/2023].

[32]August (n 1) 535.

[33]It is also called the Vienna Convention or UN Convention on the International Sale of Goods. Chuah (n 25) 175.

has been ratified[34] by as many as 96 states,[35] and the number is increasing.[36] Its popularity as a set of substantive rules[37] makes it a noteworthy example of harmonising transnational law.[38] Notably, almost all of the disputes between Chinese contracting parties and other foreign parties, settled under the China International Economic and Trade Arbitration Commission (CIETAC) were governed by the CISG.[39]

Studying the history of CISG requires first studying the convention on which CISG is based, namely ULIS. The comparison between these Conventions is tantamount to understanding how the new law differs from its predecessor. The nucleus of this research is the disparity between the two Conventions associated with the provisions of the remedies and obligations of the parties which are

---

[34]Harold Berman, 'The Uniform Law o International Sale of Goods: A Constructive Critique' (1965) 30(2) Law and Contemporary Problems, 355; Graeme Cooper, 'The Reclamation Rights of Unpaid and Unsecured Sellers in International Trade' (1987) 17 Columbia Business Law Review 31.

[35]See <https://uncitral.un.org/en/texts/salegoods/conventions/sale_of_goods/cisg/status> [accessed 4/9/2023].

[36]See Paul Berman, 'From International Law to Law and Globalization' (2005) 43 Columbia Journal of Transnational Law 490.

[37]Schwenzer; Kee, 'Global Sales Law: Theory and Practice', in Ingeborg Schwenzer; Lisa Spagnolo, Towards Uniformity: The 2nd Annual Maa Schlechtriem CISG Conference (Hague, Eleven International Publishing 2010) 157.

[38]See ibid 157.

[39]Gotanda, 'Yin & Yan: A Comparison of Monetary Remedies in International Investment and Transnational Commercial Disputes', in Schwenzer; Spagnolo (n 36) 49-51.

regarded as the core of the international sale of goods contract.[40] Many Articles of both Conventions run in parallel[41] but others are different as CISG changed, supplemented and eliminated some parts of the text of ULIS. This study discusses in detail the evaluation of hidden aspects of such variance between the CISG and ULIS, and estimates the procedural, technical, conceptual and textual differences by scrutinising the Articles of both Conventions. It investigates whether the amendments to ULIS by CISG result in the best outcome, and one that is compatible with international sale and represents a compromise between different legal systems. This comparison determines the drafters' intentions of CISG on one hand, and analyses CISG's preferential approach for a particular issue on the other.

The literature lacks such a comparison between CISG and ULIS, which is important in order to fully appreciate the CISG. This comparison is conducted by elucidating the Articles in both conventions, supported with the case-law on CISG and hypothetical scenarios on ULIS to clarify the discrepancy between both regimes. ULIS suffers from a scarcity of precedents, whereas interpretation of the CISG is relatively easy to analyse due to accessible databases.[42] This research demonstrates the efficiency of

---

[40]The ULIS' system in displaying the remedies was not adopted by CISG. In ULIS, each obligation was attached by the appropriate remedy for its breach, in order to make the trader directly aware of the lawful consequences for such breach. See: Bianca; Bonell (n 16) 329; Shafiq (n 30) 166. Nevertheless, the repetition of the remedial provisions makes such system inconvenient and difficult to understand so that, in CISG, the remedies was united in one section for each the seller's obligations part and the buyer's obligations part. Bianca; Bonell (n 16) 329.

[41]Such as the majority of the Articles in connection with delivery of the goods, for example, Article 20, 22 & 23 of ULIS and Article 33 of CISG.

[42]Jeffrey Hartwig, 'Schmitz-Werke GMBH & Co. v. Rockland Industries Inc. and the United Nations Convention on Contracts for the International Sale of Goods (CISG): Difference and Developing International Legal Norms' (2003) 22 Journal of Law and Commerce 97-98.

CISG, which may result in many countries leave sticking 'their domestic sales law as a tail to international kite'[43] in order to participate and be an effective participant of the international community in global trade.

Because the subject is associated with certain concepts like 'internationality', 'selling' and 'goods', it is necessary to include a synopsis to explain these hypotheses under the two Conventions.

1.1. Internationality

ULIS and CISG will not be applied unless the contract is international. ULIS takes into account cumulative factors in order to specify the 'internationality' and therefore its application.[44] The first requirement of internationality is that the parties' businesses are physically based in different countries, although these countries do not have to be contracting states.[45] Second, the contract should either involve the movement of goods across borders, the issuance of the offer and acceptance in different states, or the delivery of the goods in a state other than the state in which the contract was formed.[46] On the other hand, CISG stipulates that it will be applied only either when parties' business places exist in different contracting states,[47] or when the rules of private law lead to the application of the domestic law of contracting state. [48] Reliance solely on the parties' business places could cause uncertainty at the time of formation of the contract, especially when a party has relevant business places in different countries.[49] Moreover, the norms of ULIS are a more persuasive representation of a truly international con-

---

[43]Honnold, 'The Uniform Law' (n 27) 332.

[44]László Réczei, 'The Area of Operation of the International Sales Conventions' (1981) 29 American Journal of Comparative Law 514.

[45]Honnold, 'The Uniform Law' (n 27) 333.

[46]ULIS Art. 1; ibid 274; Shafiq (n 30) 63-66; Rosett (n 30) 274.

[47]CISG Art. 1; Réczei, (n 43) 517.

[48]CISG Art. 1; August (n 1) 536.

[49]Rosett (n 30) 269.

tract[50] while CISG may encompass national contracts concluded in one country and involving goods which do not entail shipment[51] just because the parties' business places are in different contracting states. The CISG's aim is to expand its scope and effectively cover all sales of goods that might be regarded as international.[52]

1.2. Sale of Goods

Neither of the Conventions defines the concept of 'sale' or 'goods'. Instead, the Conventions list categories of sale that are out of scope. Consumer purchasing and selling by auction are excluded under CISG[53] but not under ULIS.[54] CISG also precludes sales where the predominant part of the seller's obligations is merely to supply labour or other services,[55] for example, if a hotel supplies a factory with wood and materials in order to manufacture beds. Here, the function of the factory is limited to making such goods.[56] This contract does not constitute a sale under CISG, but it does ULIS, which does not exclude such a sale from its scope. In this way, ULIS has a wider scope for application than CISG.

---

[50]Bradley Richards, 'Contracts for the International Sale of Goods: Applicability of the United Nations Convention' (1981) 69(1) Iowa Law Review 218.

[51]Rosett (n 30) 275.

[52]ibid 275.

[53]CISG Art. 2(a) & (b); Schwenzer; Hachem, 'General Provisions: Article 2', in Ingeborg Schwenzer, Commentary on the UN Convention on the International Sale of Goods (CISG) (Oxford University Press 2014) 49-54; Martin Davies; David Snyder, International Transactions in Goods: Global Sales in Comparative Context (Oxford University Press 2014) 48; August (n 1) 537.

[54]ULIS Art. 5; John Honnold, 'The Draft Convention on Contracts for the International Sale of Goods: An Overview' (1979) 27(2/3) The American Journal of Comparative Law 227.

[55]CISG Art. 3(2).

[56]Shafiq (n 30) 73.

1.3. The Importance of the Paper and the Reason for the Length of the Study

As Pearl S. Buck emphasised, 'if you want to understand today you have to search yesterday.' From this standpoint, it is important to be aware of the historical aspect of any international treaty, thus scrutinising the antecedent of the UN Convention on Contracts for International Sale of Goods (CISG), namely The Convention relating to a Uniform Law on the International Sale of Goods (The Hague 1964, ULIS) is vital. The paper is nearly 15,000 words and this length is justifiable, as the work is a comparative study between two international Conventions, as it is crucial in order to understand, for example, the general principles upon which the newer Convention (CISG) is based, and to know the history by examining all the articles of the former and the newer Conventions. This method also serves to illustrate what adjustments and amendments have occurred to ULIS. As the American historian David McCullough emphasised, 'history is who we are and why we are the way we are', therefore this facilitates the recognition of what CISG is and why it is the way it is today. This approach is to avoid the abandonment of amendments and to adopt the opposite, as George Santayana clarified, 'those who do not remember the past are condemned to repeat it.' This study is inevitable for the sake of assessing and evaluating the two Conventions side-by-side and to conclude a final judgement regarding whether the change has been effective. This imperative evaluation between the present and the past enables the reader to observe the development of innovative ideas in the practical side of sale of goods all over the world.

1.4. The Author's Role in Advancing Knowledge: Novel Contributions:

This study focuses on the differences between the two Conventions, which is more important than knowing the similarities. Take this simple example: when X paints their wall the colour green, and after a while 'they change the colour to beige. This informs you that green was probably not the best option and should be avoided. In contrast, where the colour is the same, there is no additional information to be acquired. This applies to the named Conventions, as the differences can provide the interpreter with benchmarks or criteria about the mentality and the philosophy of the current Convention (CISG). Hypothetical and real cases are provided to highlight the disparities between the two Conventions, and analytical evaluation is provided after each contrast to assess the attitude of each Convention.

To the author's knowledge, there is no single work about this comparison which covers the mentioned areas in the study, such as, inter alia, obligations of the seller, including delivery of goods, conformity of goods, and claim of third parties, in addition to buyer's duties, remedies for a seller's breach of contract, embracing specific performance and the seller's right to cure, and obligations of the buyer, remedies for the buyer's breach of contract, anticipatory breach, instalment contract and damages.

2. Obligations of the Seller

According to both Conventions, the seller is duty-bound to deliver the commodities to the buyer as agreed in the terms of the contract.[57]

2.1. Delivery of Goods

Under CISG, if the parties have not specified the place for the handing-over of goods, and the contract imposes upon the seller the carriage of goods;[58] the seller will fulfil their commitment if they hand the goods over to the first inland carrier for transmis-

---

[57]CISG Art. 30 & ULIS Art. 18. Herbert Bernstein; Joseph Lookofsky, Understanding the CISG in Europe (London, Kluwer Law International 2003) 72; Michael Bridge, Benjamin's Sale of Goods (London, Thomson Reuters 2014) 423. It is required under both CISG and ULIS to deliver documents related to the sale of goods transaction, like a health certificate, bill of lading and certificate of origin to the buyer. CISG Art. 34 & ULIS Art. 50. J. Abdulaziz, Obligation of Conformity in the Contract of the International Sale of Goods: According to Vienna Convention (Cairo, Dar Anahda Alarabia 1996) 278. CISG adds a condition that does not exist in ULIS, namely that if the seller delivered defective documents before the agreed time, the seller might rectify such defects (e.g. typing errors or missing signatures), when two criteria are met: a) the rectification occurs before the agreed date for the delivery, and b) this does not cause unreasonable inconvenience or unreasonable expense to the buyer. CISG Art. 34. Stefan Kröll; Loukas Mistelis, Pilar Viscasillas, UN Convention on Contracts for the International Sale of Goods (CISG) (Oxford, Hart Publishing 2011) 480; Joseph Morrissey; Jack Graves, International Sales Law and Arbitration (Netherlands, Kluwer Law Internationa 2008) 165; Robin Burnett, Law of International Business Transactions (Sydney, The Federation Press 1999) 21. Some scholars affirm that such a condition replicates Article 37 of CISG about the early delivery of goods. Kröll et al (n 56) 481. It would be more precise if the latter Article encompassed goods and documents instead of duplicating the same issue in two Articles.
[58]Such as in the terms of C & F and CIF Contracts.

sion to the buyer.[59] For example, from their premises in Birmingham, a seller hands over the goods to an overland carrier to transport them by truck to an establishment in London, where the goods will be packed.[60] The goods are then handed over again by a truck to a maritime carrier in a British port to ship them to the port of Marseille to be transported by road to Paris, where the buyer's firm is located. The seller, under CISG, carried out their commitment at the point of the delivery of the goods to the British port, not when handing over the goods to the overland carrier in the seller's premises.[61] ULIS does not designate exactly which carrier the seller should hand the goods over to;[62] whether, as in the above example, the overland carrier in London, the maritime carrier in the British port, or the overland carrier tasked with transporting the goods to Paris.[63] Determining the time at which the obligation of delivery is accomplished is very important as it consequently decides when the liability of risk transfers to the buyer.[64] Under CISG

---

[59]Bianca; Bonell (n 16) 251; Larry Dimatteo; Lucien Dhooge; Stephanie Greene; Virginia Maurer; Marisa Pagnattaro, International Sales Law: A Critical Analysis of CISG Jurisprudence (Cambridge University Press 2005) 104-105.

[60]Vincent Heuze, La Vente Internationale de Marchandise (Paris, Librairie Generale de Droit et de Jurisprudence 2000) 327.

[61]Shafiq (n 30) 137; Schwenzer, Commentary (n 52) 929.

[62]ULIS Art. 19(2). It states that delivery will be affected from the moment of handing over the goods to '...the carrier for transmission to the buyer.'

[63]John Honnold, Documentary History of the Uniform Law for International Sales: The Studies, Deliberations and Decicions that led to the 1980 United Nations Convention with Introductions and Explanations (Netherlands, Kluwer Law and Taxation Publishers 1989) 115; André Tunc, Commentary on the Hague Conventions of 1st July 1964 on the International Sale of Goods and on the Formation of Contracts of Sale (Pace Law School Institute of International Commercial Law 1998) 46. Available: <https://www.unidroit.org/english/conventions/1964ulis/explanatoryreports/ulis-ulfc-explanatoryreport-e.pdf> [accessed 29/9/2023]

[64]CISG Art. 67(1) & ULIS Art. 19(1), 19(2) & 97(1). Honnold, Documentary (n 62) 454.

the risk passes to the buyer when the goods are handed over to the first carrier,[65] or when the goods are delivered to the place at the date agreed in the contract.[66] Thus, if the goods deteriorated after the time of the delivery, the seller is not liable. Under ULIS, the obligation of delivery is not complete unless the goods conform to the contract.[67] This can result in consequences for the seller as they would bear all responsibility[68] at these later stages in transit when the buyer would best-placed to take care of the goods, assess the damage and protect them from any further possible harm.[69] This applies even if the goods perished in transit or in possession of the buyer. CISG separates the obligation of delivery and the obligation of conformity of goods.[70] Therefore, the seller performs their obligation of delivery even if the goods are defective[71] and any loss or damage that occurred after this point is borne by the buyer unless such loss is otherwise proven to be the liability of the seller.[72] The seller is responsible for all 'pre-shipment' or 'pre-delivery' defects.[73] However, it is difficult for the buyer to prove that the goods were damaged before shipment or that the loss did not occur in transit.[74] In such circumstances it is advisable to resort to

------

[65]CISG Art. 67(1) & ULIS Art. 99(1), which mentioned merely 'carrier'. Burnett (n 56) 14.

[66]CISG Art. 67(1) & 69 & ULIS Art. 97(1).

[67]ULIS Art. 19(1). Ronald Graveson; Ernest Cohn; Diana Graveson, The Uniform Laws on International Sales Act 1967 (London, Butterworths 1968) 63-64; Viejobueno (n 28) 224.

[68]ibid 224.

[69]Muna Ndulo, 'The Vienna Sales Convention 1980 and the Hague Uniform Laws on International Sale of Goods 1964: A Comparative Analysis' (1989) 38(1) International and Comparative Law Quarterly 18.

[70]Honnold, Documentary (n 62) 121 & 250.

[71]Bianca; Bonell (n 16) 253.

[72]CISG Art. 66 & 67(1). Ingeborg Schwenzer; Christiana Foun- toulakis; Mariel Dimsey, International Sales Law: A Guide to the CISG (Oxford, Hart Publishing 2012) 491-492.

[73]Burnett (n 56) 14.

[74]Bianca; Bonell (n 16) 489.

INCOTERMS'[75] contracts, such as Cost Insurance and Freight (CIF) contracts which require insurance of the goods.[76] The seller may also issue a certificate from a neutral company to prove the conformity of goods before exportation.[77] In the earlier example it might be more appropriate to refer to the first maritime carrier as a point for delivering the goods, thereby avoiding passing the risk to the overland carrier in London on the grounds that the seller is closer to the goods than the buyer and can assess any damages and pursue compensation if needed. Furthermore, if the goods were ruined during the transmission from London to the British port because of an accident, this would be a local issue that the seller can deal with, being more familiar with the legal system in their country.

CISG, unlike ULIS, adds that a seller's retention of documents pertaining to the goods does not affect the risk passing to the buyer.[78] An example to illustrate: a seller is contracted to deliver medical machines to the port of their buyer, but with the stipulation that the title and documents of the goods would not transfer until full payment. The goods are damaged in transit. The court refuses to attach the risk to the seller because neither the title nor the documents are transferred to the buyer.[79] Thus, CISG is more practical as it places great importance on the physical possession than the actual ownership of the goods in terms of who bears the risk in

---

[75]International Commercial Terms sponsored by International Chamber of Commerce. This kind of terms seeks to bring harmonisation by persuasion instead of imposition. Schwenzer; Spagnolo (n 36) 162; Mckendrick (n 17) [9].

[76]P.S. Atiyah; John Adams; Hector MacQueen, Atiyah's Sale of Goods (England, Pearson Education Limited Publishing 2010) 430-431 & 415; Chuah (n 25) 82-84.

[77]Atiyah et al (n 75) 195; Michael Bridge, The International Sale of Goods (Oxford University Press 2013) 121.

[78]Art. 67(1).

[79]St. Paul guardian insurance company et al v Neuromed medical systems & support et al (26/3/2002) 00 Civ 9344 United States Federal District court (New York)
(2002). Morrissey; Graves (n 56) 160.

transit. This is more suitable to international sales whereas the link between ownership and bearing risk is more appropriate to domestic sales. Moreover, CISG, unlike ULIS, obliges the seller, at the buyer's request, to provide all of the information necessary to facilitate the issuing of insurance,[80] such as the names and addresses of insurance companies in the seller's country.[81] This provision is beneficial to encourage insurance the goods so that any dispute concerning damages to the goods can be shifted away from the parties and to the insurance company. Additionally, it enhances the cooperation between the parties and expedites international transactions.

A question arises: if the goods are sold in transit, when does the risk transfer to the buyer? Assume that on 1st September, a perfume shipment was sent from the Marseille port to be handed over to an Egyptian company. On 5th September, while the goods were in transit, the Egyptian company sold them to a Greek corporation. The ship's captain therefore received an order to send the goods to Piraeus port.[82] The Greek corporation received the goods, but they were defective. Under ULIS, the risk passes retroactively to the Greek corporation from the time the goods were handed over to the carrier, i.e. 1st September.[83] Therefore, the seller (the Egyptian company) is not liable for the non-conformity of goods.[84] This provision was criticised on the grounds that it is unjust to transfer the risk before the contract of sale was made.[85] However, if the Egyptian company knew about the goods' defects before dealing with the Greek company,[86] the passage of goods to the buyer would be from the moment of concluding the contract while the

---

[80]Bianca; Bonell (n 16) 260.

[81]Shafiq (n 30) 137.

[82]ibid 213-214.

[83]ULIS Art. 99(1). Bianca; Bonell (n 16) 496.

[84]Viejobueno (n 28) 225.

[85]Bianca; Bonell (n 16) 496.

[86]Bad faith seller.

goods were in transit.[87] A seller could exploit this provision of ULIS by selling defective goods, which is a particular problem in circumstances where the buyer may be unable to determine when the defects occurred. CISG determines the time that the delivery was completed[88] as the time of concluding the contract associated with the goods sold in transit,[89] i.e. 5th September in the above example. Alternatively, according to CISG, the transfer of risk occurs at the point of handing over the goods to the carrier[90] when the parties intended to refer to such point (when, for instance, endorsing the goods' insurance which covers all the risk from the time the goods are loaded on the ship).[91] Some scholars advocate the approach of ULIS and argue that it is too troublesome to pinpoint the time of the goods' loss or damage in transit, such as determining the moment when sea water may have leaked into the goods' containers.[92] However, CISG's rationale is more judicious on two grounds: First, in many cases the deterioration of goods can be verified by experts to determine the exact time of the damage, i.e. whether it occurred before or after concluding the contract.[93] The time of a disaster, such as a fire or collision, can also easily be pinpointed through technological communications.[94] Second, an international convention should not protect a seller operating in bad faith as this could undermine confidence in international trade.[95]

---

[87]ULIS Article 99(2). A. Sultan, Passage of Risk in the Contract of International Sale of Goods (Cairo, Dar Anahda Alarabia 2010) 185-186.

[88]Therefore, passing the risk to the buyer.

[89]CISG Art. 68. Ndulo (n 68) 19.

[90]CISG Art. 68; Burnett (n 56) 15.

[91]Schwenzer et al, International Sales Law (n 71) 498-499. Nevertheless, if the seller knows, or ought to have known about the defects, the seller is liable for such defects or loss. CISG Art. 68; ibid 499.

[92]Sultan (n 86) 188- 189; Bernstein; Lookofsky (n 56) 109-110.

[93]Abdulaziz (n 56) 131.

[94]Heuze (n 59) 331.

[95]Consequently, global growth, mutual interdependence and universal prosperity will recede. Bossche; Zdouc (n 3) 6-20.

2.2. Conformity of Goods

Under both Conventions, the seller should provide the buyer with goods matching the quantity, quality and description required in the contract.[96]

2.2.1. Goods' Characteristics

ULIS rules that the buyer's claim of non-conformity shall not be taken into consideration if such non-conformity is trivial or is within the limits of tolerance ratios.[97] For example, a slight difference in the weight of cotton is customary.[98] CISG does not explicitly mention such exemption provision. Some scholars hold that mentioning such a clause in CISG would be superfluous, especially as minor discrepancies[99] in goods are overlooked under customary international law and such law should, in any case, be applied pursuant to Article 9 of CISG.[100] Other scholars find that ignoring such difference in conformity of goods is pursuant to the principle of 'good faith',[101] which is regarded as one of the important general principles on which CISG is based.[102] On the other hand, some scholars are reluctant to impose the principle of good faith, due to

---

[96]Bianca; Bonell (n 16) 269; Bernstein; Lookofsky (n 56) 75; Graveson et al (n 66) 72; Bridge, Benjamin's (n 56) 551.

[97]ULIS Art. 33(2).

[98]Shafiq (n 30) 147.

[99]Schwenzer, Commentary (n 52) 569.

[100]Customary international law is compulsory, unless the parties agreed otherwise. Shafiq (n 30) 147.

[101]The Vienna Convention on the Law of Treaties 1969 states in Article 26: 'Every treaty in force is binding upon the parties to it and must be performed by them in good faith'. See: Spagnolo, 'Global Sales Law', in Schwenzer; Spagnolo (n 36) 191.

[102]Peter Schlechtriem, Commentary on the UN Convention on the International Sale of Goods (CISG), Translation: Geoffrey Thomas (Oxford University Press 1998) 65; Bernstein; Lookofsky (n 56) 92-93; Goode et al cited Kastely (n 13) 283.

the absence of express provision which imposes such obligation.[103] Others affirm that slight dissimilarity should not be disregarded because some contracts rely on totally intact goods.[104] For instance, a company is contracted to manufacture and sell statues with the characters' names provided on the statue. On the delivery date, the buyer refused to pay the price on the grounds that the names appeared on the left side. The seller did not make a transgression, as long as the contract mentioned nothing about the place of the names and, furthermore, this difference could be deemed inconsequential. However, at the time of the negotiations, the buyer explained that the aim of the statues is to glorify noble characters, meaning that it is important for their identities to be conspicuous. Because of these subtleties, under CISG the importance of the defects is left to the decision-makers on a case-by-case-basis.

i) Packaging the Goods

Article 35(1) of CISG includes a kind of conformity that is not referred to by ULIS: the conformity of packaging the goods.[105] This kind of conformity is crucial as the commodities in international sales usually cross long distances with a variety of means of transportation that expose them to different weather conditions. With such conditions, most cases of lack of conformity in goods are attributed to defective packaging failing to protect them.[106] CISG points out three sequential steps to be followed. First, the goods should be packed according to the requirements of the contract. Second, in the absence of such stipulation, the goods should be packaged consistently with the usual manner of packaging for similar commodities[107] e.g. flowers wrapped in cellophane.[108] Finally,

---

[103]Goode et al (n 13) 279; Bridge, The International Sale of Goods (n 76) 509.
[104]Bridge, Benjamin's (n 56) 551&723.
[105]CISG Art. 35(1). Bianca; Bonell (n 16) 276-277.
[106]Abdulaziz (n 56) 98.
[107]Bianca; Bonell (n 16) 277.
[108]Also, electronic devices are placed in cardboard boxes surrounded by nylon cushions. Shafiq (n 30) 146.

the goods must be packed in an adequate manner to preserve them,[109] especially if the goods are new and unique,[110] e.g. made from briquette or ore.[111] In the case of **Conservas La Costeña v Lanín San Luis**, a contract was agreed to deliver 8,000 tins of canned fruit from Argentina to Mexico, but when the buyer received the goods, they discovered that the goods were damaged. The tribunal found that the seller was liable for this because they failed to package the goods in a way that was sufficient to protect them, as dictated by CISG.[112] It is problematic to claim under ULIS that the non-conformity of goods is due to inadequate packaging. Nevertheless, Article 35(1) of CISG may conflict with Article 9 of CISG, which imposes an obligation to apply the usage of international trade widely known, as some commodities, like ores and minerals,[113] are customarily shipped unpackaged. The question is whether the judge should rely on the usage of international law[114] or the obligation of packaging the goods,[115] in the case of defective goods being received due to packaging faults.

ii) *Sale by Sample*

If contracted to sale by sample, the goods should be compatible with the characteristics of the sample sent by the seller.[116] CISG

---

[109]In the absence of a usual manner.

[110]Bianca; Bonell (n 16) 277.

[111]ibid 277.

[112]CISG Art. 53(2) (d). Conservas La Costeña S.A. de C.V. v Lanín San Luis S.A. & Agroindustrial Santa Adela S.A. (29/04/1996) M/ 21/95 COMPROMEX, Comisión para la Protección del Comercio Exterior de Mexico; Morrissey; Graves (n 56) 179.

[113]Ajay Menon, '8 Major Types of Cargo Transported Through the Shipping Industry' (5/5/2021) <https://www.marineinsight.com/types-of-ships/8-major-types-of-cargo-transported-through-the-shipping-industry/#:~:text=Dry%20bulk%20cargo%20refers%20to,carriers%20include%20ores%20and%20minerals.>

[114]CISG Art. 9.

[115]CISG Art. 35(2)(d).

[116]ULIS Art. 33(c) & CISG Art. 35(2)(c).

classifies the consignment of the sample as a guarantee of the quality of the purchased goods to be received, unless it is agreed otherwise.[117] Under ULIS, the consignment of a sample does not mean that the seller will provide similar goods.[118] Instead, a sample is merely an indication of the nature of the goods offered.[119] It would have to be agreed, either explicitly or implied, that goods with the same features of the sample would be delivered.[120] Under ULIS, if the parties contracted to sell goods by sample, the seller should provide in the delivered goods all qualities found in the sample, and they are responsible for non-conformity even if the buyer is aware (or could not be unaware) of the goods' defects at the time of signing the contract.[121] Conversely, CISG excludes the seller from liability for any lack of conformity, even in the case of sale by sample and where the buyer was aware of non-conformity when signing the contract.[122] The approach of ULIS is preferable because it relies on the contract, which contains a clause to sell by sample, which provides the measure of conformity. The seller cannot evade their contractual obligations by arguing that the buyer knew the goods' defects at the time of concluding the contract.[123] Additionally, Article 35(3) of CISG facilitates the seller's ability to prove the buyer's presumed knowledge of lack of conformity when articulating that the buyer '...could not have been unaware...'.[124] This impedes the contractual balance between the parties which is a critical principle of international conventions.[125] Furthermore, under CISG, a problem can arise if the parties agreed on common descriptions of the goods in the contract, such as the colour but

---

[117]Schwenzer, Commentary (n 52) 582-583; Dimatteo et al (n 58) 117; Davies; Snyder (n 52) 190.

[118]ULIS Art. 33(c).

[119]Bridge, Benjamin's (n 56) 597.

[120]ULIS Art. 33(c).

[121]ULIS Art. 36. Honnold, Documentary (n 62) 123.

[122]CISG Art. 35(3).

[123]Heuze (n 59) 256-258.

[124]CISG Art. 35(3).

[125]For example CISG Art. 74. Abdulaziz (n 56) 228.

definite specifications, such as the shape, were referenced by the sample without mention in the contract.[126] Parol evidence is usually not admissible to show that the sale is by sample.[127] This may be considered a legal loophole that gives the seller the green light to confirm the characteristics of their own goods according the buyer's general needs.[128] It is recommended to forewarn the buyer, when CISG is applicable, that sale by sample should be mentioned in the contract (specifying, for example, the number of the sample agreed on) to avoid conflict with the seller over which qualities of the sample were agreed on.

iii) Uses of Goods

Under both Conventions, the goods must be appropriate for ordinary use[129] which means the goods should have the basic characteristics of typical goods in order to be tradable.[130] ULIS states that goods should be suitable to their ordinary use (in singular) in contrast to CISG which refers to ordinary purposes (in plural).[131] If the goods referred to are used vehicles, for example, which are used for multiple purposes including travelling, loading and racing, it is sufficient under ULIS that only the main ordinary purpose is available i.e. the ability of the vehicles to move, whereas CISG takes into account the existence of all ordinary purposes of such vehicles. CISG enables the buyer to reject goods if they are not suitable to one of their purposes.

---

[126]Atiyah et al (n 75) 205.

[127]ibid 205; Rod Andreason, 'MCC-Marble Ceramic Center: The Parol Evidence Rule and Other Domestic Law under the Convention on Contracts for the International Sale of Goods' (1999) Brigham Young University Law Review, 358.

[128]CISG Art. 65(1) & ULIS Art. 67(1).

[129]CISG Art. 35(2)(a) & ULIS Art. 33(1)(d). Honnold, 'The Uniform Law' (n 27) 337.

[130]Davies; Snyder (n 52) 194-195.

[131]CISG Art. 35(2) (a) & ULIS Art. 33(1) (d).

Moreover, under both Conventions, the goods should be suitable for any other particular purposes[132] which the buyer intends to use the goods for. Therefore, Jeeps should not only be operational, but should also be able to sustain extreme climate conditions and withstand dense sand if, at the time of concluding the contract, the buyer expressly or implicitly informed the seller that they would use the Jeeps for oil exploration in the deserts.[133] CISG, unlike ULIS, supplements a requirement that the buyer should demonstrate their reliance on the seller's skills to supply the goods according their particular requirement.[134] Thus, CISG imposes a liability on the buyer to search for a specialist in manufacturing the concerned goods for a particular use.[135] Consequently, if the seller is just an intermediary,[136] or if the buyer knows of the limited capabilities[137] of the seller to meet their requirements, the buyer cannot claim afterwards that the goods did not conform to their particular purpose.[138] However, it is difficult to refer to the buyer's non-reliance if the seller is a manufacturer or when they use effective inducement to persuade the buyer to agree to purchase the commodity.[139] In these cases reliance will be presumed.[140] Finally, if the contract elaborated on the specific purpose desired by the buyer, the seller cannot afterwards deny their obligation to provide such goods, on the basis that the buyer did not rely on their skills, as consent between the parties is legally binding. ULIS instead relies on the seller's declaration of refusal if the buyer's private purpose for the goods outweighs the seller's capacity. Dependence on the

---

[132]CISG Art. 25(2) (b) & ULIS Art. 33(1) (e).
[133]Shafiq (n 30) 145.
[134]The second sentence of CISG Art. 35(b). Davies; Snyder (n 52) 195-196; Bridge, The International Sale of Goods (n 76) 549.
[135]Schwenzer, Commentary (n 52) 581-582.
[136]ibid 582.
[137]Atiyah et al (n 75) 194.
[138]Shafiq (n 30) 145.
[139]Atiyah et al (n 75) 194.
[140]ibid 194.

seller's refusal is preferable on the grounds that the seller is best equipped to estimate their own abilities.

2.2.2. Claim of Third Persons

Both Conventions necessitate that the goods sold should be free from the rights or claims of a third person, unless the buyer agrees to buy the goods with these claims.[141] Such rights and claims can incur the buyer significant expenses for litigation, protection and indemnification.[142] CISG enlarges the explanation of the third person's claim, specifically claims related to industrial and intellectual property.[143] Industrial property claims includes brand, trademark ownership or patenting, whereas intellectual property claims encompass copyright, translation rights and composing.[144] For example, if a bookshop in Cairo bought copies of a French book that was printed and published in Paris and the author came into conflict with the publisher in France about the copyright, they may threaten the bookshop with legal action which might end in a ban on selling such books and expropriating them.[145] The seller (the bookshop) is liable for such a claim of copyright infringement only if they knew or could have been unaware of the issue at the time of concluding the contract.[146] CISG, unlike ULIS, limits the seller's liability through specifying the relevant laws to determine whether the seller is in breach or not: first, the law of the country where the goods will be resold or used, in case of contemplating such countries at the time of concluding the contract; or in other cases, and second, the law of a country where the buyer's business is located.[147] However, the seller is not liable for the claim if: (i) the

---

[141]ULIS Art. 52 & CISG Art. 41. Bianca; Bonell (n 16) 318; Bridge, The International Sale of Goods (n 76) 557.
[142]Bianca; Bonell (n 16) 318.
[143]CISG Art. 42, 43 & 44. Honnold, Documentary (n 62) 426.
[144]Shafiq (n 30) 161.
[145]ibid 162.
[146]CISG Art. 42(1).
[147]Art. 42(1) (a) & (b). Honnold, Documentary (n 62) 427.

buyer knew about the existence of such a claim, or they are culpable of lack of knowledge; or (ii) the seller complies with the buyer's technical specifications, which infringe the intellectual and industrial property rights.[148] Such an Article does not exist in ULIS. The increasing significance of intellectual and industrial property rights made by the drafters of the CISG enacts a distinctive regime for such claims.[149]

2.2.3. Time of Assessing Conformity

The seller is liable for all defects that existed in goods before transferring the risk to the buyer[150] even if such defects did not appear until the goods were used by the end consumer.[151] The carrier of the goods does not necessarily have the knowledge or experience to examine and verify the goods. Moreover, such examination may require opening the packages of goods, which would in turn compromise the quality of packaging and expose the goods to risk of damage.[152] CISG only requires the defects to exist before passing the risk to the buyer in order to blame the seller, regardless of who caused the defect.[153] Conversely, ULIS protects the buyer's right to claim non-conformity when the defects occur before[154] the delivery, and when such defects are the result of the seller's own actions (or their agent's).[155] To illustrate, if the goods are a shipment of wheat, and two days after receiving them the buyer discovers that they are full of mites,[156] the seller is liable for the non-conformity

---

[148]Art. 42(2) (a) & (b). Kröll et al (n 56) 657-658.

[149]ibid 648.

[150]CISG Art. 36(1) & ULIS Art. 35(1).

[151]Heuze (n 59) 276.

[152]Abdulaziz (n 56) 138; Albert Kritzer, Guide to Practical Applications of the United Nations Convention on Contracts for the international Sale of Goods, (Boston, Kluwer and Taxation Publishers 1989) 292.

[153]CISG Art. 36 (1). Abdulaziz (n 56) 139.

[154]When ULIS indicated in Art. 35(2) that the seller is liable for the 'consequences' of unconformity.

[155]ULIS Art. 35(2).

[156]ibid 141.

of the goods under CISG,[157] but they are not under ULIS. The seller is not liable under ULIS because the defects, which **appeared** after passing the risk to the buyer, are not due to the seller's acts[158] even if such mites **existed** before the risk was passed to the buyer. CISG expands the sphere of the seller's responsibility when adopting such objective criterion[159] to close off the possibility of the seller selling defective goods. Furthermore, CISG extends the seller's liability for the deterioration pof goods where this occurs (not appears) beyond the passage of risk[160] in two scenarios. The first is if the non-conformity is due to a breach of seller's obligations,[161] such as the contract containing a term obligating the seller to send their experts to periodically check the goods and train the buyer's employees about the best methods for using the sold goods.[162] The seller is liable for any technical malfunction in the devices sold that occur after delivery to the buyer, if the defects occur as a result of their failure to perform the above obligations. The second is if the contract contains a term of guarantee[163] to ensure the characteristics of the goods within a period of time[164] then the seller should warrant any defects that may appear in that time.[165] Such provision does not exist in ULIS. Practically, the guarantees and additional obligations of the seller are contractual obligations, i.e. they are expressly mentioned in the contract and there is no need to replicate such terms in the Convention.

---

[157]Bianca; Bonell (n 16) 286.

[158]ibid 284.

[159]ibid 284.

[160]Shafiq (n 30) 149.

[161]CISG Art. 36(2). Kröll et al (n 56) 545.

[162]Shafiq (n 30) 149.

[163]Atiyah et al (n 75) 288.

[164]Such as a 12-month guarantee. Bridge, Benjamin's (n 56) 723.

[165]Kröll et al (n 56) 546; Dimatteo et al (n 58) 107-108.

2.2.4. Buyer's Duties

Both CISG and ULIS stipulate two conditions for the buyer's claims alleging non-conformity to be considered valid:[166]

(i) Inspection of Goods

ULIS imposes on the buyer the responsibility of examining the goods 'promptly'[167] once they are handed over. Therefore, the buyer should immediately inspect the goods after obtaining them.[168] CISG requires examination of the goods to take place in '… as short a period as is practicable in the circumstances.'[169] The two Conventions presuppose the rapid inspection of goods to accurately identify the evidence of imperfections, prevent the defects from exacerbating[170] and eliminate any concerns about terminating the contract.[171] The two Conventions have practical differences due to the different phrasing they use. Impediments beyond the buyer's control,[172] such as a general strike, can be taken into account under CISG to determine the time taken to examine the goods.[173] Additionally, some circumstances are considered through CISG (but absent from ULIS),[174] which may lengthen or shorten the procedure of the inspection, such as: the quantity of the goods; their packaging;[175] their nature; whether they are complex machinery or

---

[166]Dimatteo et al (n 58) 77; Bernstein; Lookofsky (n 56) 87.

[167]ULIS Art. 38(1). Eörsi (n 29) 335.

[168]Graveson et al (n 66) 58.

[169]CISG Art. 38(1).

[170]John Honnold, Uniform Law for International Sales under the 1980 United Nations Convention (Boston, Kluwer and Taxation Publisher 1991) 328; Dimatteo et al (n 58) 76.

[171]Shafiq (n 30) 151.

[172]As a juristic reasoning by analogy to CISG Art. 79(1). Kritzer (n 151) 304.

[173]ibid 304. Alternatively, arrival of the goods just before public holidays may make it difficult to find a specialist in the inspection process at this time. Dimatteo et al (n 58) 78.

[174]ULIS Art. 38(1). Eörsi (n 29) 335.

[175]Dimatteo et al cited Garro; Luzern (n 58) 78.

simple devices; and the country of the buyer, including whether it is a developing country or a big industrial city.[176]

In cases where the buyer resells the goods to a third person,[177] under ULIS the buyer cannot defer the inspection until the goods reach the new destination; only if the goods are re-dispatched without trans-shipment.[178] This requirement is harsh on the buyer as, in practice, it is normal that the resale of goods entails them to be shipped to another destination.[179] CISG permits deferral of the inspection of goods, even in cases of trans-shipment, until the goods reach the new destination,[180] and stipulates instead that the buyer should have no reasonable opportunity to examine the goods before this time.[181] To illustrate, in a contract made between a German company and a US company to sell books, the buyer did not examine the goods (due to their packaging), and exported them to other buyers, who discovered that these books were different to the ones that they expected. The court would accuse the original seller of the non-conformity.[182] This would not be the case under ULIS because the goods were trans-shipped, which would require the buyer to check them upon receipt. However, it is impractical to open the packaging of the goods to check their conformity if they are then going to be transported again to be resold to other buyers.[183] Thus, changing the means of transportation does not necessarily give a buyer reasonable opportunity to examine the

---

[176]Alejandro Garro, 'Reconciliation of Legal Traditions in the U.N. Convention on Contracts for the International Sale of Goods' (1989) 23(2) International Lawyer 470.

[177]Shafiq (n 30) 153.

[178]Bianca; Bonell (n 16) 295.

[179]ibid 295.

[180]ULIS Art. 38(3) & CISG Art. 38(2). Dimatteo et al (n 58) 81.

[181]Bianca; Bonell (n 16) 295.

[182]Louis Lafili; Franklin Gevurts; Dennis Compbell, Survey of the International Sale of Goods (Boston, Kluwer and Taxation Publishers 1986) 110.

[183]Honnold, Uniform Law (n 169) 327-328.

goods.[184] Hence, ULIS is bound to be too seller-friendly in this respect.[185]

(ii) Notice of Non-Conformity

Under ULIS, the buyer should notify the seller 'promptly' of any lack of conformity after examining the goods.[186] This was replaced in CISG by a 'reasonable time'.[187] The formulation of CISG is more flexible as the reasonable period may vary depending on the type of goods.[188] If the goods are food products, faster notification is required than if the goods are, for example, clothes.[189] CISG, unlike ULIS, exempts the buyer from the notification within a 'reasonable time' if the buyer has an acceptable excuse for their failure to inform the seller about the non-conformity,[190] such as a strike which halts telecommunications, internet disconnection in the buyer's area, or if the nature of the goods calls for inspection by a foreign specialist identify any defects.[191] In such circumstances, the buyer is limited to using specific remedies, such as price reductions or claims for damage, 'except for loss of profit'.[192] However, the concept of 'reasonable excuse' lacks clarity.[193] Some scholars assert that the court may regard the buyer's unfamiliarity with the notice system as a reasonable excuse.[194] It is hard to take into account the purely personal circumstances of the buyer as a reasonable excuse, such as the buyer's illness or lack of experience of the

---

[184]ibid 327-328.

[185]Kröll et al (n 56) 561.

[186]ULIS Art. 39(1). Burnett (n 56) 20.

[187]CISG Art. 39(1). Schwenzer, Commentary (n 52) 622-623.

[188]Heuze (n 59) 270-271.

[189]ibid.

[190]CISG Art. 44. Morrissey; Graves (n 56) 216; Dimatteo et al (n 58) 91.

[191]Abdulaziz (n 56) 218.

[192]CISG Art. 44. Morrissey; Graves (n 56) 216; Viejobueno (n 28) 222.

[193]Garro cited schlechtriem, 'Reconciliation of Legal Traditions' (n 175) 472.

[194]Kröll et al (n 56) 674.

international commerce requirement, especially as they may fabricate their ignorance or hardship to justify their non-notification. Therefore, it must be estimated by a reasonable person in the same circumstances. Some commentators argue that this provision is biased towards the buyer, therefore the seller should protect themselves by adopting a clause in the contract that eliminates any excuses for failure to provide notice.[195] However, CISG achieves parity between the parties as it allows the buyer to justify why they did not notify the seller, which is compatible with trade practice. ULIS adds a third stipulation on the buyer in order to claim non-conformity; the seller (or their agents) must be invited to examine the goods to prove their defects.[196] CISG eradicated this rule, which is regarded as a harsh technicality[197] that is inconsistent with international trade practice.[198]

Both Conventions contain a limitation cut-off period[199] in which the buyer loses the right to resort to lack of conformity if they did not notify the seller within two years from the date of handing over the goods.[200] Such a period is related to hidden defects that cannot be detected immediately.[201] Notwithstanding, such period is too long for food goods and may be too short for industrial equipment, so it is advisable to include a guarantee period in the contract that corresponds to the nature of the goods.[202] CISG excludes the two-year period if the contractual guarantee duration is longer or short-

---

[195]Dimatteo et al (n 58) 91.

[196]The second sentence of ULIS Art. 39(2). Graveson et al (n 66) 76-77.

[197]Honnold, 'The Uniform Law' (n 27) 335.

[198]Schwenzer, Commentary (n 52) 622-623.

[199]David Fagan, 'The Remedial Provisions of the Vienna Convention on the International Sale of Goods 1980: A Small Business Perspective' (1998) 2 The Journal of Small and Emerging Business Law 328.

[200]CISG Art. 39(2) & ULIS Art. 39(1). Dimatteo et al (n 58) 77; Bernstein; Lookofsky (n 56) 94-96.

[201]Kröll et al (n 56) 612-613.

[202]Abdulaziz (n 56) 217; Bernstein; Lookofsky (n 56) 95.

er than such period,[203] while ULIS permits lengthening the two-year period but not shortening it,[204] although the need to curtail such period is necessary for some kinds of perishable goods, such as flowers.

ULIS adds another condition in which the buyer loses their right to claim non-conformity if they have not determined which remedy they should use within one year from the date of notifying the seller of the goods' defects.[205] This period is too long as the buyer would be expected to decide on the course of action within a reasonable time after notifying the seller about non-conformity in order not to leave the seller concerned over the fate of the goods and to avoid disputes occurring after lengthy periods of time, during which the evidence may be lost.[206]

3. Remedies for a Seller's Breach of Contract

3.1. Specific Performance

'Specific performance' occurs in cases where a buyer demands the actual terms of the contract to be met and refuses to be compensated payment of damages in place of this.[207] If a seller's breach of the contract is because the goods suffer from a lack of conformity, the

---

[203] Art. 39(2). Morrissey; Graves (n 56) 216; Fagan (n 198) 331.

[204] Last sentence of Art. 39(1) CISG and last sentence of Art. 39(1) ULIS. Abdulaziz (n 56) 216-217; Graveson et al (n 66) 76-77.

[205] ULIS Art. 49(1).

[206] Shafiq (n 30) 159; Graveson et al (n 66) 81.

[207] Anthony Kronman, 'Specific Performance' (1978) 45(2) The Chicago Journal of International Law 352. Such a remedy is generally recognised in civil law countries, contrary to common law systems, which allow specific performance in limited cases. Schwenzer et al, International Sales Law (n 71) 465. Notably, the buyer cannot resort to specific performance in both conventions when the court, settling the dispute, would not do so under its domestic law in relation to similar local contracts. CISG Art. 28 & ULIS Art. 16. Bernstein; Lookofsky (n 56) 119-120; Bridge, Benjamin's (n 56) 684.

buyer can ask for specific performance, thereby requiring substitute goods from the seller, or repair of the defective goods.[208] ULIS, unlike CISG, forbids the buyer from resorting to such a remedy if the buyer is reasonably able to purchase alternative goods.[209] Suppose that a Spanish buyer is contracted with an Austrian seller to sell bars of silver and, on the agreed date of delivery, the seller refuses to perform on the grounds that the market price of silver in Austria increases.[210] Under CISG, the buyer can ask for specific performance, but ULIS prevents the buyer from doing so if they are able to purchase such silver bars at a reasonable price from an Italian seller instead, for example. This could allow the seller to neglect their obligations to deliver a contract, if the merchandise they are selling can be accessible from other market sources.[211] Furthermore, ULIS restricts the repair of defective goods to the producer and manufacturer,[212] which is favourable to the seller.[213] CISG requires two conditions in order to demand substitute goods. First, the defects of goods must constitute a fundamental breach,[214] as the replacement involves sending new commodities to the buyer and returning the defective ones, which causes significant expenses to the seller.[215] Second, the buyer has a duty to return the goods in a similar condition to which they received them.[216] This reflects the diligence with which CISG seeks to balance the parties' interests.

---

[208]CISG Art. 46(1) & ULIS Art. 24(1)(a); 26(1); 30(1); 31(1); 41(1) & 42(1). Ndulo (n 68) 15.

[209]ULIS Art. 25. Bianca; Bonell (n 16) 334; Mahdi Zahraa; Abdullah Ghith, 'Specific Performance under the Vienna Sales Convention, English Law and Libyan Law' (2000)15(3) Arab Law Quarterly 309.

[210]Bernstein; Lookofsky (n 56) 119.

[211]Zahraa; Ghith cited Honnold (n 208) 307.

[212]Art. 42(1)(a). Abdulaziz (n 56) 424.

[213]See CISG Art. 46(3). ibid 431.

[214]CISG Art. 46(2). Bianca; Bonell (n 16) 335.

[215]ibid 335. Shafiq (n 30) 175.

[216]CISG Art. 82(1).

3.2. The Seller's Right to Cure

The seller may fail to perform their obligations in the case of delayed delivery or otherwise handing over of non-conforming goods.[217] The seller has a right to remedy any fault from their side after the delivery date passes.[218] CISG necessitates that such remedy must be at the seller's expense, while ULIS requires not causing the buyer unreasonable expense.[219] In this way, under CISG, the seller is the only responsible party for remedying their breach of the contract, while under ULIS, the buyer may participate materially in the seller's rectification, either directly or indirectly, such as by using their time and resources to fix the defective goods. CISG stipulates that the seller should address such problems within a reasonable period.[220] In the case of **Tetracycline**, the court refused to exercise the seller's right to remedy their performance because the defects needed a considerable amount of time to be fixed, which would cause substantial damages to the buyer.[221] This condition is significant as, under ULIS, which does not require such prerequisite, the seller may take too long to fix their performance, impeding the rapidness of international transactions. The non-existence of such a condition makes the buyer forced to grant the seller an additional period of time to fulfil their obligations, which should be of reasonable length (according to Article 27(2), 31(2) and 44(2) of ULIS, and Article 47 of CISG) in all cases related to non-fundamental breach, in order not to give the seller an opportunity to take an excessive length of time (more than a reasonable time) to resolve the matter.[222]

---

[217]Schwenzer, Commentary (n 52) 734-735; Burnett (n 56) 25-26.
[218]ULIS Art. 44(1) & CISG Art. 48(1). Morrissey; Graves (n 56) 220; Bernstein; Lookofsky (n 56) 73.
[219]ULIS Art. 44(1) & CISG Art. 48(1).
[220]CISG Art. 48(1).
[221]Tetracycline HCL case (23/6/1995) – 271 C 18968/94 Amtsgericht München (Local Court Munich) Germany; Morrissey; Graves (n 56).
[222]Schwenzer, Commentary (n 52) 737; Kröll et al (n 56) 714.

ULIS states that if defective goods represent a fundamental breach of contract and the buyer has not promptly declared the contract avoided, the seller may exercise their right to remedy their performance,[223] whereas CISG refers to Article 49, associated with the avoidance, as if it encourages terminating the contract when the breach is fundamental.[224] For example, a seller sends a notice to a buyer apologising for not dispatching the goods on 15th September, as specified in the contract, and informing them that the day of dispatch will be the 20th September instead. In response, the buyer may exploit the situation to avoid the contract, not allowing the seller to attempt to resolve the situation.[225] This is the opposite of the principle adopted by CISG to reduce resorting to avoidance.

3.3. Reduction of Price

A buyer may request a reduction in the price of the goods because of the seller's inadequate performance.[226] CISG confines this mechanism to the non-conformity of goods,[227] but under ULIS, the buyer can use this remedy for a deficiency of any of the seller's obligations.[228] There are perceived contradictions in ULIS as it allows the technique of price reduction to be used in relation to any breach on one hand, but exempts the breaching party from compensation if they are facing highly difficult circumstances on the

---

[223]ULIS Art. 44(1).

[224]Article 48(1) of CISG started with the words: '[s]ubject to article 49'. Article 49 is related to the cases permitted to avoid the contract. Bianca; Bonell (n 16) 348.

[225]Shafiq (n 30) 180.

[226]A. Kheir, Contracts for the International Sale of Goods: Through Vienna Convention and the efforts of United Nations Committee of International Trade Law (UNCITRAL) and International Commercial Chamber(ICC) (Cairo, Dar Alnahda Alarabeya 1994) 95; Burnett (n 56) 25.

[227]CISG Art. 50. August (n 1) 575.

[228]ULIS Art. 46.

other.[229] Therefore, a seller that may be facing adverse circumstances preventing them from being able to deliver the goods by the agreed time can be exempted from compensation. At the same time, ULIS gives the buyer the opportunity to reduce the price by as much as, if not more than, the equivalent amount of inoperative compensation.

The calculation of a price reduction is different in the two Conventions. CISG compared the value of the delivered (defective) goods and the hypothetical value of the conforming goods at the time of delivery.[230] It is not always an easy task to determine the actual value of the goods at the time, especially if there is no common price or no similar products on the market.[231] ULIS estimates the price reduction according to the difference between the actual value of the goods, not the contracted price, at the time of concluding the contract and the defective goods.[232] A true assessment of the goods' value at the time of concluding the contract could especially difficult if this date is in the distant past.[233] For example, in a contract to sell and deliver cheese for $90,000 to the buyer's port, the goods were found to be worth $95,000 according to the market value at the time that it concluded.[234] The seller dispatched the goods, but during the journey, the ship was interned for two months due to unexpected hostilities. The ship finally reached its destination, but the quality of the cheese had suffered and was now

---

[229]ULIS Art. 74(1). Eric Bergsten; Anthony Miller, 'The Remedy of Reduction of Price' (1979) 27(2/3) The American Journal of Comparative Law 273.

[230]CISG Art. 50. Schwenzer, Commentary (n 52) 774; Dimatteo et al (n 58) 138-139.

[231]Heuze (n 59) 413.

[232]ULIS Art. 46. Abdulaziz (n 56) 446.

[233]It is challenging to know the circumstances surrounding the product, such as supply and demand elements, in that time.

[234]In an ex-ship contract, the seller is responsible for the transit risks. Atiyah et al (n 75) 421.

worth $20,000. The value of the conforming goods at the time of the delivery amounted to $100,000.[235] The reduction in value is $80,000 ($100,000 minus $20,000), so under CISG, the buyer would pay the amount agreed in the contract minus this reduction ($90,000 minus $80,000), which comes to $10,000. However, the reduction in value under ULIS is $75,000, as it uses the market price of the goods at the time of agreeing the contract, not the agreed price in the contract ($95,000 minus $20,000). Therefore, the buyer would pay $15,000 ($90,000 minus $75,000).

Under CISG, the buyer may consider which choice would be more advantageous to them; the remedy of the damages or the price reduction, and in doing so may depart from neutrality and disrupt the balance between the parties' interests. If the value of goods at the time of delivery increases, the buyer will likely resort to the price reduction, but if the value declines, they will instead claim damages.[236] However, CISG supplements a restriction that the buyer is not allowed to reduce the price if the seller offers to remedy their performance and the buyer refuses.[237] This restriction reduces the buyer's ability to abuse this mechanism. However, this can also be used in a non-fundamental breach with no definition of such a breach,[238] giving the buyer an opportunity to ask for a price reduction without a valid reason or for something that is inconsequential to them,[239] such as delivering goods with a different colour. Some commentators argue that the difference in colour does not constitute a hindrance to discharging the goods on the market,[240] while others regard it as a breach of the contract.[241]

---

[235]Honnold, Uniform Law (n 169) 335-336.

[236]Morrissey; Graves (n 56) 282; Bergsten; Miller (n 228) 274.

[237]CISG Art. 50.

[238]Schwenzer, Commentary (n 52) 773; Atiyah et al (n 75) 297-300.

[239]Especially if the two countries are equally efficient in the industry.

[240]The same applies to a difference in the goods' origin. C. Witz, Les Premières Applications Jurisprudentielles du Droit Uniforme de la Vente Internationale (Paris, L.G.D.J 1995) 85-87.

[241]Fagan (n 198) 326.

4. Obligations of the Buyer

The buyer is under a duty to pay the price and accept the delivery of goods in accordance with the terms of the contract.[242]

4.1. Price of Payment

In order to ensure that the buyer will pay the owed purchase price,[243] both Conventions oblige the buyer to take steps and undertake procedures for the preparation of paying the price.[244] ULIS gives examples for this provision, such as opening a documentary credit or giving a banker's guarantee.[245] CISG is satisfied with only mentioning the provision's aim and deletes such examples to clarify that these procedures are not compulsory but are dependent on each case.[246] ULIS states that payment and delivery are concurrent conditions.[247] Consequently, the buyer may refuse to pay until the seller has delivered the agreed goods.[248] This stipulation is not expressly stated in CISG because it corresponds to internal sale.

In the absence of the purchase price being stated in the contract explicitly or implicitly, the purchase price will be determined under CISG,[249] according to the price generally charged at the time of concluding the contract for similar goods sold under comparable circumstances.[250] It is difficult to know which price should be

---

[242]Bridge, Benjamin's (n 56) 481.

[243]Kröll et al (n 56) 804.

[244]CISG Art. 54 & ULIS Art. 69.

[245]ULIS Art. 69.

[246]Schwenzer, Commentary (n 52) 812; Dimatteo et al (n 58) 93-95.

[247]ULIS Art. 71. Bridge, The International Sale of Goods (n 76) 563.

[248]ibid 563-564.

[249]The purchase price could be determined implicitly if the price was specified according to the previous contract, or by referring to the price of the stock exchange. Shafiq (n 30) 194.

[250]CISG Art. 55. Kröll et al (n 56) 814-815; Bernstein; Lookofsky (n 56) 101-102.

charged if there are no identical goods in the market,[251] such as unique works of art.[252] A further complication is that CISG does not pinpoint in which geographical market the general price should be taken from. Under ULIS, the purchase price will be specified pursuant to 'the price generally charged by the seller...' at the time of concluding the contract.[253] This criterion is neither practical nor neutral as the buyer is left with no protection.[254] However, some scholars assert that it is the buyer's duty to discover this price and they cannot allege at a later time that such price is unfair or unexpected.[255]

This provision contradicts two other clauses. First, the contract is valid when the price is not specified, but the validity of the contract is excluded from the sphere of both Conventions.[256] Second, there is a proviso in both Conventions that requires the offer to be sufficiently definite,[257] and the price constitutes an essential element of a contract.[258] One commentator asserts that the Conventions exaggerate in seeking to preserve the contract by filling the gap of the price, as it is regarded as the heart of the contract.[259] Reliance on external factors does not necessarily mean that such factors reflect the parties' intentions.[260]

4.1.1. Place of Payment

CISG expressly refers to the place of payment agreed in the contract and, in the absence of such an agreement, the buyer should

---

251 Bianca; Bonell (n 16) 403.

252 Shafiq (n 30) 196.

253 ULIS Art. 57. Eörsi (n 29) 334.

254 Schwenzer, Commentary (n 52) 816.

255 Graveson et al (n 66) 86.

256 CISG Art. 4(a) & ULIS Art. 8 of ULIS. Bianca; Bonell (n 16) 401.

257 CISG Art. 14(1) & ULF Art. 4(1).

258 ibid 402.

259 Dimatteo et al (n 58) 96-97.

260 ibid 97; Kröll et al (n 56) 813.

pay at the seller's place of business or at the place where goods are handed over.[261] ULIS does not refer to the parties' consent but instead obliges the buyer to directly pay the price at the seller's place of business or at the place where goods are handed over.[262] CISG gives great consideration to the will of the parties, which is compatible with both international trade and the circumstances of each contract. However, some commentators assert that there is no need to set a place of payment because payment in the form of notes and cheques is an anachronism in the technological age, and payment should instead be carried out electronically, supported by a secure, robust and available system.[263]

4.1.2. Time of Payment

Under CISG, if the contract does not mention the time of payment, the buyer should pay the price when the seller put the goods 'at the buyer's disposal',[264] i.e. when the buyer is able to possess and use the goods without hindrance. The goods do not have to be seized physically, as long as the seller notifies the buyer about placing them in a specific place.[265] ULIS requires the price to be paid when the seller delivers the goods.[266] From the wording of ULIS, it seems that the buyer is not obliged to pay until they receive the goods, so placing the goods at the buyer's disposal is not enough to qualify. Such interpretation is evidenced by the statement in ULIS

---

[261]CISG Art. 57(1). Bianca; Bonell (n 16) 412.

[262]ULIS Art. 59(1).

[263]Stig Mjolsnes; R. Michelsen, 'Open Transnational System for Digital Currency Payments' (1997) 5 Proceedings of the Thirtieth Hawaii International Conference on System Sciences 198-207. Both Conventions are silent about the currency in which the buyer should pay. Kröll et al (n 56) 806; Bridge, The International Sale of Goods (n 76) 563. Some scholars advocate payment in the currency of the buyer's place of business. Bridge, The International Sale of Goods (n 76) 395. Others assert paying in the currency of the seller's place of business. Shafiq (n 30) 197.

[264]CISG Art. 58(1); Burnett (n 56) 14.

[265]Shafiq (n 30) 134.

[266]ULIS Art. 71. Graveson et al (n 66) 92.

that the buyer should be given an opportunity to examine the goods before payment:[267] such examination can only be practiced when the goods are physically with the buyer. However, CISG has an exception for not giving the buyer the opportunity to examine the goods, namely when such examination is incompatible with the procedures of the delivery, such as placing the goods at the buyer's disposal. CISG is more suitable to international sales, especially when the contract is 'Ex-Works',[268] as the seller delivers the goods when they place them at their factory or at another named place, such as a warehouse.[269]

In cases where the contract involves carriage of goods, ULIS permits the seller to either postpone dispatching the goods until the price is paid or to dispatch them while reserving the right to retain the goods during transit until they receive payment.[270] CISG thus allows the seller to not hand over the goods to the buyer, after dispatching them, depending on payment.[271] The seller cannot therefore wait for payment before dispatching the goods.[272] This reflects the contractual equality between the parties, where the seller cannot be granted a secure procedure to ensure they receive payment before sending the goods while the buyer, having paid, not sure whether or not the goods will be dispatched. Furthermore, CISG omits the clause related to retaining the right to dispose of the goods during transit by the seller because, in many cases, the risk is transferred to the buyer once the goods are loaded on board, par-

---

[267]ULIS Art. 71.

[268]The seller has to make the goods available at the agreed place. Ex Works (EXW) <https://www.incotermsexplained.com/the-incoterms-rules/the-eleven-rules-in-brief/ex-works/> [accessed 8/10/2023).

[269]International Chamber of Commerce, 'Incoterms® 2020' <http://www.iccwbo.org/products-and-services/trade-facilitation/incoterms-2010/the-incoterms-rules/> [accessed 8/10/2023]; Atiyah et al (n 75) 408.

[270]ULIS Art. 72(1).

[271]CISG Art. 58(2).

[272]Bianca; Bonell (n 16) 420-421.

ticularly if the contract is Free on Board (FOB).[273] Thus, it is unreasonable while passing the risk to buyer, who bears all costs thereafter, to permit the seller to act freely with the goods.

ULIS indicates that if the contract entails payment when documentation is exchanged, the buyer is not authorised to defer payment until they examine the goods.[274] CISG makes no mention of such a case because, on one hand, it reflects the general provision of the parties' autonomy to organise their affairs[275] and, on the other hand, this generally occurs when the contract is Cost Insurance and Fright (CIF), which compels the seller to arrange and pay for transport and insurance.[276] Hence, once the seller has handed the documents, i.e. insurance and freight, to the buyer, the total price is payable unless agreed otherwise.[277]

4.2. Taking Delivery

This obligation consists of two parts, outlined below.[278]

4.2.1. Buyer Facilitating Delivery

Under ULIS, the buyer should undertake everything that is 'necessary' to enable the seller to hand over the goods.[279] That means the buyer is obliged to carry out all these actions, even if this is beyond what a reasonable buyer would expect. Such things might relate to the regulations of the seller's country, such as checking the con-

---

[273]'Free On Board (FOB)' <http://www.incotermsexplained.com/the-incoterms-rules/the-eleven-rules-in-brief/free-board/> [accessed 8/10/2023]; Atiyah et al (n 75) 408.

[274]ULIS Art. 72(2).

[275]Goode et al (n 13) 271.

[276]'Cost Insurance and Freight (CIF)' <http://www.incotermsexplained.com/the-incoterms-rules/the-eleven-rules-in-brief/cost-insurance-freight/> [accessed 8/10/2023]; Bridge, The International Sale of Goods (n 76) 130 &184.

[277]Shafiq (n 30) 200.

[278]Honnold, Documentary (n 62) 437.

[279]ULIS Art. 65. Ndulo (n 68) 17.

formity of goods by the buyer before shipment according the seller's jurisdiction. However, recognising that the buyer should not be expected to know all the regulations of their sellers. CISG modified such a clause so that buyers should carry out all actions that are 'reasonably expected' to facilitate delivery.[280] This means buyer is expected to comply with administrative formalities, such as acquiring an import license according to the legislations of their country.[281]

4.2.2. Taking Over Goods

ULIS imposes on the buyer the responsibility of 'actually' taking the goods over,[282] meaning that the buyer, or their agents, should physically receive the goods.[283] However, the original buyer would not take the goods over if they resell them to a third party before the seller's notification of placing the goods in their factory[284] and the ultimate buyer will receive them instead. CISG removed the word 'actually' to reflect compatible with such practice in international trade.[285]

In the Ex-Works contract, risk passes to the buyer when they take the delivery from the seller's place of business[286] at the agreed time.[287] However, if the buyer fails to take the delivery at this agreed time, when will the risk transfer to the buyer? If the agreed date for taking the goods was between 1st October until 25th Oc-

---

[280]CISG Art. 60.

[281]Schwenzer et al, International Sales Law (n 71) 456. Also, in cases where the contract is FOB, the buyer is expected to arrange and pay for carriage to enable the seller to deliver the goods. ibid 455; Chuah (n 25) 54.

[282]ULIS Art. 65.

[283]Honnold, Documentary (n 62) 437; Atiyah et al (n 75) 301-302; Burnett (n 56) 13.

[284]The contract is ex-works. Chuah (n 25) 35.

[285]CISG Art. 60(b).

[286]Atiyah et al (n 75) 420; Burnett (n 56) 13.

[287]CISG Art. 69(1) & ULIS Art. 97(1). Bernstein; Lookofsky (n 56) 102-103.

tober and the buyer took the delivery on 22nd October, the risk would transfer to the buyer from that date under both Conventions.[288] However, there is a difference if the buyer fails to take the delivery in this period of time. Under ULIS, the risk would pass to the buyer on the final day, in this case 25th October.[289] This provision may encourage the buyer to postpone taking over the goods until 25th in order to keep the risk in the hands of the seller as long as possible. CISG, by contrast, passes the risk for the goods to the buyer on the first day, i.e. 1st October, in the case that they do not take over the goods within the agreed period.[290] This encourages the buyer to acquire the goods punctually. Nevertheless, it is crucial to require the buyer to notify when the goods are placed at their disposal, even if the contract mentions the date, for fear that the buyer may wrongly assume that the seller delayed in placing the goods. Moreover, the contract may specify the delivery date without indicating the latest date on which delivery of the goods can be taken. Thus, it is beneficial to recommend that the buyer takes over the goods when the seller places them at the buyer's disposal, or within a reasonable time from this point in time. CISG mentions another scenario, namely, placing the goods with a third party[291] or in a warehouse.[292] The risk passes to the buyer when the buyer is notified that the goods are placed in the location.[293] This case does not depend on the goods being taken over but, instead, on the seller's unilateral act of placing them somewhere.[294] This rule is efficient for the seller as the goods are not with them to preserve the goods until the buyer picks them up at a later time.

---

[288]ULIS Art. 97(1); Article 69(1).
[289]ULIS Art. 98(1).
[290]CISG Art. 69(1).
[291]Schwenzer et al, International Sales Law (n 71) 502.
[292]Schwenzer, Commentary (n 52) 939.
[293]CISG Art. 69(2).
[294]Schwenzer, Commentary (n 52) 939.

5. Remedies for the Buyer's Breach of Contract

5.1. Specific Performance

Under CISG, if the buyer has not performed any of their obligations, such as paying the purchase price or taking the delivery, the seller may turn to the court, asking for specific performance.[295] ULIS stipulates two restrictions to the use of this provision: (i) this mechanism is restricted to non-payment of price, thus the seller cannot ask for specific performance in relation to other obligations of the buyer;[296] and (ii) the seller is not entitled to require the buyer to pay the price when it is reasonably possible for them to resell the goods.[297] The conduct of ULIS is analogous to the common law systems, which tighten the application of this remedy, whereas CISG enlarges such application in a way that is equivalent to civil law jurisdictions.[298]

5.2. Avoidance

Under ULIS, the buyer's failure to pay the price on the agreed day amounts to a 'fundamental breach' of contract and the seller should either ask the buyer to pay the price[299] or declare the contract

---

[295]CISG Art. 62. A court belonging to common law jurisdiction has the right to refuse resorting to such a remedy. CISG Art. 28 & ULIS Art. 16. Schwenzer et al, International Sales Law (n 71) 464; Viejobueno (n 28) 210. This provision is regarded as a compromise between civil and common law systems. Garro, 'Reconciliation of Legal Traditions' (n 175) 459.

[296]ULIS Art. 61(1).

[297]ULIS Art. 61(2).

[298]Bianca; Bonell (n 16) 452.

[299]In case the component court permits specific performance according to Article 16 of ULIS.

avoided.[300] This decision should be within a reasonable time, otherwise the contract will be automatically avoided.[301] This provision enables the buyer, when the contract is no longer profitable to them, to avoid the contract by merely withholding the price. Such a hypothesis is not found under CISG. CISG prohibits the seller from declaring the contract avoided with respect to any failure of the buyer's obligations, as long as the buyer has paid the price.[302] CISG supplements two exceptions to the above rule.[303] First, in cases where the buyer was late in performing any of their obligations, and on that grounds the seller declares the contract avoided before they 'know' that the performance was fulfilled.[304] This provision enlarges the avoidance remedy. This remedy should not be restricted to 'late' performance but, instead, to 'undue delay'. CISG uses a solely subjective criterion which relies on the seller's knowledge, where the seller may pretend that they do not know that the late performance is fulfilled in order to terminate the contract. Thus, objective criterion should be added according to a reasonable person's knowledge.[305] Second, on the assumption that the buyer refuses to perform any of their obligations, the seller is permitted to declare the contract avoided within a reasonable time af-

---

[300]ULIS Art. 62(1).

[301]ibid. In cases where the seller certainly wants to avoid the contract, there is no need to declare avoidance within a reasonable time as long as the fate of the contract, ultimately, will be ipso facto avoidance. Thus, this provision would be more judicious if it required the seller to ask the buyer to pay the price within a reasonable time, otherwise the contract would be automatically avoided from the moment the reasonable time expired.

[302]CISG Art. 2(2). Schwenzer et al, International Sales Law (n 71) 477.

[303]CISG Art. 64(2).

[304]For example, the buyer may pay the price but appears late to take the delivery. The seller can declare the contract avoided, even though the buyer may actually take over the goods but does not inform the seller of this. Schwenzer, Commentary (n 52) 904.

[305]ibid 904.

ter they knew[306] of such refusal.[307] Determining whether the buyer's attitude embodied procrastination or rejection is problematic, especially when the buyer does not communicate their position.

5.3. Designating the Specifications of Goods

The parties may agree on the nature of the goods to be sold but refer specifications of details to a later time, to be clarified by the buyer. For example, a contract was concluded to sell shoes without specifying the colours, which are to be designated a month before delivering the goods.[308] The buyer may not specify the goods' features on the agreed date or after receiving a request from the seller to specify them.[309] Under ULIS, the seller may either determine the specification themselves[310] or declare avoidance directly after the buyer's failure to determine the goods' specifications.[311] CISG only permits the seller to decide on the goods' specifications, but does not allow them to avoid the contract on the basis of the buyer's failure to designate such specifications.[312] CISG exemplifies the notion of obviating the termination of the contract.[313] Practically, ULIS is preferable as in many cases the buyer would want to undertake a feasibility study in their country's market on the goods' specifications, such as the demand factor and price discrimination, so that they can maximise their profits,[314] while the seller would have no knowledge about these demands in the buyer's country. The buyer's silence may indicate an unwillingness to buy such

---

[306]Or ought to have known.

[307]CISG Art. 64(2). ibid 903; Shafiq (n 30) 205.

[308]Heuze (n 59) 296.

[309]CISG Art. 65(1) & ULIS Art. 67(1).

[310]ULIS Art. 67(1).

[311]Schwenzer et al, International Sales Law (n 71) 480-481.

[312]CISG Art. 65.

[313]Shafiq (n 30) 208; Burnett (n 56) 21.

[314]Scott Fay; Jinhong Xie, 'Probabilistic Goods: A Creative Way of Selling Products and Services' (2008) 27(4) Marketing Science 675.

goods, especially where their marketability is reduced.[315] The seller's act of specifying the goods' features and dispatching them to the buyer will most likely result in the buyer's refusal to take the delivery and pay the price.[316] Some scholars advocate that the seller should be allowed to avoid the contract, under CISG, in case of difficulty in determining the specifications, on the grounds that it constitutes a fundamental breach.[317]

ULIS stipulates that when the seller specifies the features of the goods in place of the buyer, they should provide all the specifications they are aware of and are required by the buyer[318] (i.e. real knowledge).[319] This should be in line with previous dealings or with the negotiations between the parties prior to concluding the contract. CISG requires the availability of specifications that are likely to be known by the seller[320] i.e. supposed knowledge. Under CISG, a question arises regarding whether the seller is obliged to provide goods of particular specifications that are required in the buyer's country, as long as the seller is likely to be aware of them. For instance, if the goods are a shipment of chocolate to a Middle Eastern buyer, should the goods be free from gelatin pork or alcohol, despite none of this being mentioned in the contract? Some scholars repudiate such a notion on the grounds that the seller is not expected to know other countries' requirements.[321] Others assert that the seller should provide specifications in specific cases, such as when the seller has a branch in the buyer's country, or the seller regularly exports to such a country.[322] In the Video recorders case, a seller delivered video recorders to a Swiss buyer with solely

---

[315]Shafiq (n 30) 206.

[316]Heuze (n 59) 297.

[317]Bianca; Bonell (n 16) 475-476; Kröll et al (n 56) 876.

[318]Bianca; Bonell (n 16) 476.

[319]ULIS Art. 67(1).

[320]CISG Art. 65(1).

[321]Heuze (n 59) 254-256; François Dessemontet, Convention de Vienne sur les Contracts de Vente International de Marchandises. (Lausanne, CEDIDAC 1993) 278; Chuah (n 25) 186.

[322]Morrissey; Graves (n 56) 172-175.

German instructions. It was held that the seller delivered non-comforting goods for two reasons: first, it is reasonable under such circumstances to provide the instructions with any other language spoken in Switzerland; and second, it was known to the seller that such devices would be sold in Switzerland..[323]

The benchmark of seller's knowledge under ULIS seems easier and more realistic, and is dependent on communications between the parties. CISG, however, expands the knowledge criterion to include all requirements that the seller might know. Allowing a seller to determine the specifications of the goods may lead to an imbalance between the parties' interests because such a determination could only meet the minimum requirements of the buyer to not incur expenses and to obtain the largest return on the agreed price.[324] It is useful to stipulate that the seller should render goods with specifications not less than the average.[325]

6. Common Remedies for the Breach of Contract

There are common remedies that can be applied to either a buyer or a seller's breach of contract. Initially, under both Conventions, the adjudicator is not permitted to give parties any supplementary period in which to perform their failed obligations[326] for two reasons: first, to not make the international procedures longer and more expensive;[327] and second, to not '…expose the parties to the broad discretion of a judge who would usually be of the same na-

---

[323]Video recorders case (9/5/2000) 10 O 72/00 Landgericht Darmstadt, Germany.
Chuah (n 25) 187.
[324]H. Almasri, Modern Mechanisms in International Trade (Cairo, Dar Alnahda Alarabeya 2010) 55.
[325]Bridge, The International Sale of Goods (n 76) 550.
[326]ULIS Art. 24(3); 64; CISG Art. 45(3); 61(3).
[327]Bianca; Bonell (n 16) 332.

tionality as one of the parties.'[328] However, CISG mentions that this period only disallowed if the counterparty resorts to a remedy when a breach occurs.[329] The contravening party may therefore be granted an extension period in which to perform their obligations before the other party resorts to a remedy. However, this period will be suspended when the aggrieved party uses a remedy. Some scholars are strictly against the capability of judges to grant the defaulting party such a period whether before, after or during the affected party resorts to a remedy.[330] ULIS assertively bans the provision of a supplementary period by an adjudicator in relation to any of the seller's obligations[331] but it confines this prohibition (which is associated with the buyer's obligations) to the failure to pay the price.[332] Therefore, if the buyer does not take the delivery, they may be granted such a period in which to perform their obligation. Based on the above, CISG treated the parties equally, whereas ULIS impeded the equilibrium between the parties, which may impede the achievement of neutrality.

6.1. Avoidance of Contract

It is desirable in international contracts to minimise the usage of a termination mechanism,[333] especially when they are made after arduous and expensive negotiations.[334] An avoidance penalty can be used in three cases:

---

[328]ibid cited the Secretariet's Commentary 332.

[329]Kröll et al (n 56) 685; Schwenzer, Commentary (n 52) 700.

[330]Honnold, Documentary (n 62) 428.

[331]ULIS Art. 24(3).

[332]ULIS Art. 64. Bianca; Bonell (n 16) 443.

[333]Heuze (n 59) 375; M. Omar, Paying the Price in the International Sale of Goods Contract as One of the Fundamental Obligations of the Buyer. (Cairo, Technical Office of Legal Publications) 28.

[334]See CISG Art. 81 & ULIS Art. 78. Heuze (n 59) 392-393.

6.1.1. Occurrence of Fundamental Breach

Under CISG, if a fundamental breach occurs, the affected party is permitted to use severe remedies such as avoiding the contract or asking for substitute goods.[335] Under ULIS, it is not permitted to declare the contract avoided for the mere non-conformity even if it constitutes a fundamental breach.[336] In the Spanish paprika case, the seller contracted with a buyer to supply paprika complying with the permissible qualities in Germany, but delivered the spice with much greater ratios of ethyl oxide than is allowed in the country.[337] In this example, use of the termination device under CISG is legitimate. By contrast, ULIS prevents recourse to avoidance even if it represents a fundamental breach, unless the agreed upon terms of delivery are also breached.[338] Some scholars argue that each of the previous obligations, i.e. non-conformity and breach in delivery, should separately constitute a fundamental breach,[339] while others believe that both obligations may together equate to a fundamental breach.[340] Fundamental breach should be estimated inde-

---

[335]CISG Art. 25. Ingeborg Schwenzer, 'The Danger of Domestic Preconceived Views with Respect to the Uniform Interpretation of the CISG: The Question of Avoidance in the Case of Non-Conforming Goods and Documents' (2005) 36 Victoria University of Wellington Law Review 799-801. This idea is found in ULIS as well. ULIS Art. 10. Will, 'General Provisions: Article 25', in Bianca; Bonell (n 16) 209-207. The affected party can declare the contract avoided when there is a fundamental breach. ULIS Art. 32; 43; 52(3); 52(4); 55(1) & CISG Art. 49(1). The aggrieved party should notify the default party of the desire to terminate the contract 'promptly' (under ULIS) or within a 'reasonable time' (under CISG). ULIS Art. 43 & CISG Art. 64(1)(a) & 26. Eörsi (n 29) 334.

[336]ULIS Art. 43. Abdulaziz (n 56) 393; A. Abdulhameed, The Avoidance of the International Sale of Goods contract according to the Vienna Convention of 1980 (Cairo, Dar Alnahda Alarabeya 2001) 60.

[337]Spanish paprika case (21/8/1995) 1 KfH O 32/95 District Court Ellwangen; Morrissey; Graves (n 56) 175-176.

[338]ULIS Art. 43.

[339]Abdulaziz (n 56) 393; Abdulhameed (n 335) 60.

[340]Bianca; Bonell (n 16) 360.

pendently in relation to each obligation according to the effect on the aggrieved party.

In ULIS, the breach is fundamental when the breaching party knew, or ought to have known at the time of concluding the contract, that a reasonable person in the position of the injured party would not have entered the contract because of such breach.[341] The legislator in this way merely relies on the knowledge of the breaching party to consider whether a breach is fundamental.[342] This could give the breaching party the chance to claim ignorance and, therefore, to preclude avoidance of the contract.[343] It is difficult for the injured party to prove anything to the contrary.[344] For example, an external defect in the 'bat toggle switch' of the goods is slight in value compared with the overall value of the goods, so the breaching seller may believe, at the time of concluding the contract, that it is not fundamental.[345] CISG complicates the way in which the breaching party can exonerate themselves from committing a fundamental breach[346] by asking whether a reasonable person would foresee the detrimental impact it would have on the injured party. By adding such a criterion - from an objective standpoint, the breaching party can neither excuse a lack of knowledge nor incorrect assessment on their part.[347] Suppose that a someone selling cheese uses colours and preservatives in its production, which exceed the normal quantity, which causes a problem for the buyer. Under ULIS, the seller may claim that they did not know that the buyer would not want to purchase the product with such ingredi-

---

341Tunc (n 62) 24.

342ULIS Art. 10. Graveson et al (n 66) 55.

343Schroeter, 'General Provisions: Article 25', in Schwenzer, Commentary (n 52) 412; Shafiq (n 30) 120.

344Shafiq (n 30) 120.

345Schroeter, 'General Provisions: Article 25', in Schwenzer, Commentary (n 52) 407.

346ibid 401.

347Eduardo Grebler, 'Fundamental Breach of Contract under the CISG: A Controversial Rule' (2007) 101 American Society of International Law 409.

ents, because specific percentages or health rules of such ingredients are not specified in under the contract. Under CISG, any reasonable person might foresee the dangers that might be caused by such ingredients, especially if they violate international standards. The time at which this consideration should be made is not specified in CISG[348] so one may wonder whether foreseeing the consequences of a breach should be at the time of the breach or at the time of making the contract.[349] Many scholars suggest that the relevant point of time is the time of contracting,[350] which ULIS expressly refers to.[351] However, this time is not practical as a party may commit a breach after concluding the contract[352] and never think about the consequences in the time of concluding the contract.[353] For example, if a buyer asks the seller to protect some chemical goods by maintaining the appropriate temperature during transportation, and the seller agreed, yet the goods were received in a damage state,[354] CISG and ULIS would come to different conclusions. In this scenario, the seller did not predict the breach and its consequences at the time of concluding the contract because they believed that the goods would not decompose. This does not constitute a breach under ULIS, because it depends merely on a subjective criterion i.e. on the defaulting party's prediction, without indication to the reasonable person.[355] CISG, however, makes reference to a reasonable person in addition to the seller to evaluate whether the damage to goods to goods could have been predicted. In this case, any reasonable person in the place of the seller would

---

[348]CISG Art. 25.

[349]Chuah (n 25) 190.

[350]Davies; Snyder (n 52) 367.

[351]ULIS Art. 10. Will, 'General Provisions: Article 25', in Bianca; Bonell (n 16) 220.

[352]See Graveson et al (n 66) 55.

[353]Fagan (n 198) 336.

[354]Jasmine Aldehyde case (23/2/1995) China International Economic and Trade Arbitration Commission [CIETAC]; Morrissey; Graves (n 56) 167-168.

[355]Honnold, Documentary (n 62) 416; Graveson et al (n 66) 55.

certainly predict that chemicals would be affected by the climatic conditions. CISG does not specify the time of this prediction for two reasons: (i) the terms of the contracts may be amended[356] after concluding the contract, thus what the defaulting party expected at the time of concluding the contract, would not reflect the reality; and (ii) CISG intended to exclude the time of foreseeability to pave the way for subsequent information which could appear after concluding the contract.[357] For example, a one-day delay in the delivery of goods does not constitute a fundamental breach as such, but it is so if the buyer wants to display them in an exhibition on that day in particular[358] and the seller was made aware of this (even if this was after the contract was made). However, some practical complexities could arise. Assume that a contract was signed to deliver children's snacks during September, but in August a health rule was promulgated in the buyer's country that bans any children's snacks that contain more than 10% sugar. The buyer informs the seller of this requirement at the time, but it might still be too late. Should the buyer's communication be considered the point at which the seller could predict the goods being unsuitable? This kind of issue is controversial and would benefit from the addition of a touchstone in such provision to assess the seriousness of the breach, namely the ability of the buyer to use or resell the goods even if they incur extra expenses or loss (because such losses will be compensated by the seller without the need to terminate the contract).[359]

The assessment of a fundamental breach in CISG does not only look at the foreseeability by the breaching party, but it also requires the injured party to suffer a detriment which substantially deprives

---

[356]CISG Art. 29(1).

[357]It is mentioned in Article 8(3) as 'subsequent conduct'. Schroeter, 'General Provisions: Article 25', in Schwenzer, Commentary (n 52) 180-181.

[358]Shafiq (n 30) 120.

[359]Davies; Snyder (n 52) 367-368.

them of what they had expected under the contract,[360] rather than on what the breaching party promised in the contract.[361] This is likely to also be the case when applying ULIS. For example, a supplier breaches their commitment to export raw materials consistent with the contract. The importing factory did not suffer detrimental consequences from this at first because it had sufficient raw materials for its operation, but when the materials in stock were depleted and the factory was in dire need of goods, the detriment occurred.[362] According to this scenario and under CISG, a fundamental breach arises from the moment the stocks of the materials were consumed and the buyer suffered a detriment.[363] However, under ULIS, a fundamental breach occurs from the moment the breach was committed.[364] It seems that CISG gives the seller a chance to put off their obligations when they know that the buyer does not need the goods at the exact time of the delivery. Some scholars argue that reliance on the injured party's expectations gives an easy release from the contract in the case of market price fluctuation[365] because CISG depends merely on subjective criterion, namely deprivation of what the injured party is entitled to expect.[366] This may impair the contract as a source of obligations.[367] Even the goods are intact, they may be refused by the buyer on the grounds that they do not meet their expectations. Objective criterion was not added such as '… what a reasonable person is entitled

---

[360]CISG Art. 25. Dimatteo et al (n 58) 126; Franco Ferrari, 'Fundamental Breach of Contract under the UN Sales Convention; 25 years of Article 25 CISG' (2006) 25 Journal of Law and Commerce 495; Burnett (n 56) 23; Goode et al (n 13) 297.

[361]Grebler (n 346) 409.

[362]Kheir (n 225) 86-87.

[363]CISG Art. 25.

[364]ULIS Art. 10. Honnold, 'The Uniform Law' (n 27) 344.

[365]Michael Bridge, 'Avoidance for Fundamental Breach of Contract under the UN Convention on the International Sale of Goods' (2010) 59(4) International and Comparative Law Quarterly 912.

[366]CISG Art. 25.

[367]Grebler (n 346) 411.

to expect...'. ULIS objective criterion when describing the attitude of the aggrieved party, describing a situation where '...a reasonable person ...would not have entered into the contract...'. Adding an impersonal measure may lift the threshold of expectations under the contract, exceeding those of the aggrieved party.

6.1.2. Converting to Fundamental Breach

Both Conventions permit the aggrieved party to grant an additional period of a reasonable length of time as a deadline[368] to the breaching party when they have not performed their obligation within the contractual period.[369] Under ULIS, the buyer can set the additional period for the seller in relation to any failure of performance,[370] and if this time passes without fulfilling the contractual obligation, the breach automatically becomes a fundamental breach.[371] One author describes this as a regrettable provision, saying that the avoidance remedy is a dangerous tool and should be applied exclusively to extreme problems.[372] CISG employs this mechanism solely to non-delivery.[373] This limitation reduces the chance of it being exploited by applying it to minor faults.[374] However, such a system of fixing additional time will give the party a way to terminate the contract in case of any market price fluctuation[375] to serve their own interests.[376] For instance, if the agreed date for a delivery is the 1st February and the seller could not deliver the goods on that date, the buyer could give the seller an additional period, until the

---

[368]Shafiq (n 30) 171.

[369]ULIS Art. 27(2); 31(2); 44(2); 62(2) & CISG Art. 47; 63. Shafiq (n 30) 172; Burnett (n 56) 26.

[370]Such as not delivering the goods or delivering non-conforming goods. Honnold, 'The Uniform Law' (n 27) 346.

[371]ULIS Art. 27(2); 31(2); 44(2). Bianca; Bonell (n 16) 361.

[372]Honnold, 'The Uniform Law' (n 27) 346.

[373]CISG Art. 47 (1). Schlechtriem (n 101) 176; Schwenzer, Commentary (n 52) 801-802.

[374]Bianca; Bonell (n 16) 361.

[375]Bridge, The International Sale of Goods (n 76) 912.

[376]Fagan (n 198) 342; Bridge, Benjamin's (n 56) 684.

Legal Issues Journal 10(1) 2024: 9–82. ©The UK Law and Society Association

10th February, to deliver. If the seller still could not perform the task within the additional period, the breach becomes fundamental and enables the buyer to exit the contract, even if the buyer does not actually need these goods until October. This provision contradicts the touchstone to measure the fundamental breach, which is the deprivation of the expectation of the aggrieved party under the contract as a whole rather than the contractual obligation. Additionally, this provision does not specify what 'non-delivery' is.[377] It is equal if the seller does not deliver the goods at all, or if they have seller has just not delivered a small quantity of the goods. In the latter case, it is an abuse of rights to avoid the contract as a result of this breach, therefore, consideration on a case-by-case basis should be adopted to make a decision.[378] Moreover, this provision under CISG might contradict other provisions concerning permission modifying the contract on the mere parties' agreement.[379] Thus, if the buyer gives the seller a period of time after the contractual time expired to deliver the goods, it may be unclear whether such period is considered a modification of the delivery's date or an additional period of time. Each interpretation will have totally different implications. In the case of modifying the delivery's date, the seller's failure to deliver the goods by the new date will not be converted into a fundamental breach; whereas in the case that such a duration is deemed an additional period, the default of delivery will be directly regarded as a fundamental breach. Some scholars assert that a party should set the additional period with the condition that it is a hard deadline, i.e. an obligation rather than a hope, such as 'the goods should be delivered by 1st November'. Other words cannot constitute an additional period, such as 'we hope the goods will arrive by 1st November'.[380]

---

[377]Bridge, Benjamin's (n 56) 684.
[378]Grebler (n 346) 413.
[379]CISG Art. 29(1). Kröll et al (n 56) 702-703.
[380]Schwenzer, Commentary (n 52) 726.

6.1.3. Automatic Avoidance

Under ULIS, contract avoidance may occur automatically without dependence on the parties' will[381] and without the need for notification.[382] For example, when the buyer, in case of the seller's failure to perform their obligations, purchases alternative goods,[383] or when the seller resells the goods, in case of the buyer's failure to pay the price, the contract is terminated automatically from the time of repurchasing or reselling.[384] The contract is also ipso facto avoided when the seller's failure to deliver the goods[385] at the agreed time[386] or at the agreed place[387] amounts to fundamental breach and the buyer has not exercised their right to choose a remedy within a reasonable time, or does not promptly inform the seller of their decision if they are asked to do so.[388] The breaching party may unknowingly perform their obligations because they are unaware of the intended contract avoidance.[389] This provision encourages the non-implementation of contractual commitments even when the defaulting party commits an insignificant breach for fear that it would be avoided automatically. There is therefore great uncertainty in the fate of the contract.[390] Automatic avoidance is obviated in CISG[391] because it is incompatible with the principle of

---

[381]Honnold, Documentary (n 62) 84; Eörsi (n 29) 334.

[382]Christopher Jacobs, 'Notice of Avoidance under the CISG: A Practical Examination of Substance and from Considerations, the Validity of Implicit Notice and the Question of Revocability' (2003) 64 University of Pittsburgh Law Review 417.

[383]ULIS Art. 25. Ndulo (n 68) 16. Viejobueno (n 28) 210.

[384]ULIS Art. 25 & 61 respectively. Honnold, 'The Draft Convention' (n 53) 228.

[385]ULIS Art. 51.

[386]ULIS Art. 26(1) & (2).

[387]ULIS Art. 30(1) & (2).

[388]Shafiq (n 30) 121; Honnold, Documentary (n 62) 88; Ndulo (n 68) 16-17.

[389]Jacobs (n 381) 418.

[390]Bianca; Bonell (n 16) 360.

[391]See Abdulhameed (n 335) 317.

the parties' autonomy,[392] thus avoidance always requires notification.[393]

6.2. Anticipatory Breach

If the circumstances indicate that a party will commit a breach in the future, the counterparty may either suspend their performance or avoid the contract.[394]

6.2.1. Suspending Performance

A party can suspend the accomplishment of their obligations on the grounds that incidents occur, after concluding the contract, that unequivocally signify that the counterparty will not be able to carry out their obligations as contractually required.[395] Under ULIS, such suspension cannot be utilised unless the counterparty is confronting a difficult economic situation, such as the buyer being declared bankrupt.[396] CISG broadens such incidents to include: (i) acute deficiency in a party's creditworthiness;[397] (ii) serious deficiency in their ability to perform, such as a fire in the seller's factory;[398] and (iii) a party's conduct in performing the contract, such as failure to obtain an export license or to procure materials necessary for manufacturing the goods.[399] CISG's manner is more correct on

---

[392]See CISG Art. 26. Schwenzer et al, International Sales Law (n 71) 465.

[393]Clemens Pauly, 'The Concept of Fundamental Breach as an International Principle to Create Uniformity of Commercial Law' (2002) 19 Journal of Law and Commerce 225; Ferrari (n 359) 489.

[394]CISG Art. 71 & 72 & ULIS Art. 73 & 76.

[395]CISG Art. 71 & ULIS Art. 73. Shafiq (n 30) 220-221; Burnett (n 56) 26-27.

[396]ULIS Art. 73(1). Kröll et al (n 56) 921.

[397]Bridge, The International Sale of Goods (n 76) 579.

[398]Or outbreak of war. Kritzer (n 151) 466; August (n 1) 579; Kröll et al (n 56) 921.

[399]Or failure to provide a bank confirmation. Kröll et al (n 56) 922. Shafiq (n 30) 223.

the basis that suspension is contingent on the existence of evidence of the counterparty's inability to implement their required obligations. The important thing is the result, i.e. the lack of the capacity of a party, not the reason, i.e. the financial difficulty. Therefore, if a government denies to issue an export license,[400] the buyer, under CISG, can suspend their obligation to pay, because it is clear that the goods will not be delivered to their country. Under ULIS, the buyer should probably pay the price on the grounds that such denial does not constitute economic difficulty, thus the seller may obtain export license for a third country, where the buyer should take over the goods.

6.2.2. Avoiding the Contract

A party may declare the contract avoided when it is clear that the counterparty will commit a fundamental breach in the future,[401] such as reselling the goods to another buyer who offers a higher price,[402] which could incur definite delays if the seller has to manufacture new items for the original buyer. CISG stipulates that a party that wants to activate avoidance or a suspending mechanism should first notify the counterparty and request sufficient assurances of their capability to perform the contract.[403] The party is only obliged to follow this procedure if time allows them to do so.[404] CISG does not clarify the standard time allowance in this situation and, under this ambiguity, a party may misuse or exploit this instrument. CISG imposes on the innocent party the obligation to continue their performance and not to declare avoidance when the debtor (the other party) provides assurances on delivering their commitments.[405] Under ULIS, when either party suspends their

---

[400]Harold Berman (n 33) 357.

[401]CISG Art. 72 & ULIS Art. 76. Schwenzer, Commentary (n 52) 972.

[402]Shafiq (n 30) 228.

[403]CISG Art. 71(3). August (n 1) 580; Eörsi (n 29) 335.

[404]CISG Art. 72(2).

[405]CISG Art. 71(3) & 72(2). Kröll et al (n 56) 959-960; Fagan (n 198) 337-371.

performance, it is unclear when they should resume it. Adequate assurances may be refused because there is no imposition to accept them under ULIS.[406] Furthermore, ULIS permits a party to suspend their performance or declare avoidance without any notification.[407] The counterparty may perceive this as the suspending party committing a breach of contract. Notably, under both Conventions, it may be unsuitable to suspend performance, relying merely on personal concerns and thoughts that the other party may not fulfill their contractual obligations. Otherwise, this would open the way for the party to easily liberate themselves from their contractual performance. Therefore, an objective measure should be added in relation to a reasonable person in the same circumstances.

6.3. Instalment Contract

An instalment contract supplies multiple deliveries, creating long-lasting obligations.[408]

6.3.1. General Rule

According to CISG, each delivery is an independent entity.[409] Therefore, if a party commits a fundamental breach in relation to one delivery, or instalment, the other party may declare avoidance merely in respect to that instalment.[410] To illustrate, a contract requires supplying wheat in six consecutive deliveries. The first four deliveries conform to the contract's requirements, but the fifth delivery is unfit for human consumption. The buyer can declare the contract avoided solely in respect of the fifth delivery.[411] ULIS

---

[406]Thus, despite a seller controlling a strike in their factory, the buyer may refuse to perform their obligations.

[407]Harold Berman (n 33) 357.

[408]Schwenzer, Commentary (n 52) 985.

[409]Davies; Snyder (n 52) 383.

[410]CISG Art. 73(1). Kritzer (n 151) 465. Abdulhameed (n 335) 270; Chuah (n 25) 194.

[411]Heuze (n 59) 387-388.

does not address the partial avoidance just in relation to the present delivery.[412] The approach of CISG reflects an intention to maintain the contract.

6.3.2. Exceptions

Under CISG, when a party commits a breach of an instalment, this gives good grounds to predict that future fundamental breaches will also occur,[413] thus the innocent party is permitted to avoid the contract in relation to future instalments.[414] This mechanism is available under ULIS, but it does not require clear prognosis of a future fundamental breach, instead merely stipulating the fear of failure to perform future obligations.[415] This aspect of CISG represents another example of complicating a party's ability to terminate the contract.

Under CISG, the buyer may avoid the whole contract if the entire deliveries cannot be used for the purpose indicated in the contract.[416] For instance, a contract was made with a supplier for a special kind of marble, which composed of four pieces to be dispatched in four instalments, to be used to crave a large statue. The first delivery conformed to the contract but the second delivery showed the marble to be different in colour to the first delivery, making it impossible to install the statue. This constituted a fundamental breach.[417] ULIS relies on subjective measures in order to avoid the contract entirely, by asking whether the whole contract became worthless to the injured party or not. Thus, the buyer is able to terminate the whole contract based on their claim that the contract has become worthless to them, despite the breach not be-

---

[412]Kröll et al (n 56) 970.

[413]CISG Art. 73(2). Dimatteo et al (n 58) 128-131.

[414]Schwenzer, Commentary (n 52) 989.

[415]ULIS Art. 75(1). Bianca; Bonell (n 16) 532.

[416]CISG Art. 73(3). Schwenzer et al, International Sales Law (n 71) 527-528.

[417]Shafiq (n 30) 233.

ing fundamental.[418] In the above example, the buyer may avoid the contract under ULIS because, although the quality is identical to the contract's specifications, critically, the source of the marble in the second instalment is different. The subjectivity of this criterion may permit the buyer to misuse the tool according to their interests.

7. Damages

This section addresses queries relating to calculation of damages, loss mitigation, bodily injuries and exemption from damages.

7.1. Calculation of Damages

There is a provision in both Conventions concerning how to calculate the damages in case the contract is avoided, without purchasing alternative goods or reselling the goods in question.[419] The compensation equals the difference between the price agreed upon and the current value of the goods at the time of the termination.[420] The current value, under ULIS, would be based on the market of the place in which the transaction occurs.[421] However, the transaction could be interpreted differently, either as the place of delivery or the place where the contract was concluded. CISG settles this dilemma by referring to the place, where the goods were agreed to be delivered to the buyer.[422] CISG adds a new clause that if the buyer is supposed to take over the goods, the current value of the goods would be that at the time of them changing hands, rather than the time of the contract avoidance.[423] Such a clause is impor-

---

[418]ULIS Art. 75(2). Graveson et al (n 66) 96-97.

[419]CISG Art. 76 of CISG & ULIS Art. 84.

[420]CISG Art. 76(1) & ULIS Art. 84(1).

[421]ULIS Art. 84(2). Graveson et al (n 66) 101-102.

[422]CISG Art. 76(2).

[423]CISG Art. 76(1). Kröll et al (n 56) 1029.

tant to prevent the buyer from deferring declaring the avoidance until the price of the commodity changes to their advantage.[424] The possibility of speculating in case of not receiving the goods is lessened because the buyer is restricted to declaring the termination within a reasonable time.

7.2. Loss Mitigation

The affected party should adopt measures to mitigate the loss resulting from the breach in order to obtain compensation.[425] For instance, if a contract was concluded for the sale of red apples, and the buyer instead received green apples, the buyer should mitigate the loss by reselling the non-conformed goods as soon as possible to avoid the goods perishing. CISG expands this clause by obliging the affected party to also take measures to mitigate the loss of profit on behalf of the breaching party.[426] Thus, the buyer in the aforementioned example should resell the goods at the best price possible, for the benefit of the seller. ULIS, which does not adopt this clause expansion, could be a more practical option in this case because the aggrieved party should, arguably, not take extreme measures to help the breaching party.[427]

7.3. Liability for Personal Injury

CISG excludes liability for death or personal injury that may be caused by defective goods.[428] Therefore, the seller cannot be asked for compensation for such damages under CISG, but instead seek reparation under municipal law. ULIS, by contrast, does not ex-

---

[424]Shafiq (n 30) 243.
[425]CISG Art. 77 & ULIS Art. 88.
[426]CISG Art. 77.
[427]Morrissey; Graves (n 56) 287.
[428]CISG Art. 5.

clude such liability.[429] This is preferable for three reasons, First, ULIS confines cases to damages of tort claims, with any other penalties to be arranged according to the applicable law. Second, any reasonable seller will expect the possibility of mortal damage if the goods are, for instance, gas or chemicals.[430] Finally, including such consequences in the Convention's sphere would enlarge its application, unify measures relating to damages and deter the seller from violating the terms of the contract and safety rules.[431]

7.4. Exemptions

When a party cannot perform any of their contractual duties due to an unforeseeable and unavoidable difficulty that is beyond their control, the party is exempted from liability of damages (during such impediment).[432] It is to be contested whether difficulties in terms of economic hardship, like the increase in the cost of raw materials, constitutes an 'impediment'.[433] One scholar asserts that such changes in prices are foreseeable by any seller.[434] Conversely, in Scafom International BV v Lorraine Tubes S.A.S., a court concluded that the dramatic increase in prices constitutes an impediment.[435] Economic difficulties are likely to be considered an obstacle under ULIS on the grounds that it uses the word 'circumstances', which is broader than the word 'impediment' used

---

[429]Schwenzer, Commentary (n 52) 96; Morrissey; Graves (n 56) 714.

[430]Joseph Lookofsky, 'Not Running Wild with the CISG' (2011) 29 The Journal of Law and Commerce 153.

[431]Especially if the goods are reactive substances.

[432]CISG Art. 79(1) & ULIS Art. 74(1). Schwenzer et al, International Sales Law (n 71) 584.

[433]Davies; Snyder (n 52) 332.

[434]ibid.

[435]ibid; Scafom International BV v Lorraine Tubes S.A.S. (19/6/2009) C.07.0289.N Belgian Supreme Court.

in CISG.[436] CISG supplements this provision with an important scenario, namely the exemption from liability for damages because of the conduct of a third person.[437] If a third person is engaged to perform all or some of the contractual obligations of one party,[438] but this person fails to implement their duties, does the third party's failure constitute an impediment to the original party which relieves them of liability? Assume that an Egyptian car manufacturing company contracted with a Moroccan enterprise to export cars in June. The Moroccan enterprise demanded tires with certain specifications to suit the nature of the area where the goods are supposed to be used. Consequently, the Egyptian company resorted to using a third party, i.e. a company that specialises in producing tyres, to supply such tyres in April. A fire then broke out at the tyre company, making it impossible for them to fulfil the commitment to manufacture the required tyres by the agreed date. This resulted in a failure of the Egyptian company to perform its obligations.[439] To exempt the Egyptian company from liability of damages under CISG, it should first prove that the non-performance of the third party was unpredictable and out of the control of the Egyptian company and, second, that the fire was an unpredictable and unavoidable event for the tyre manufacturing company itself.[440] CISG stipulates this twofold proof on the grounds that the Egyptian company cannot be exempted from liability to pay damages due to the impediment of the third party, especially if it can ask the

---

436Aburima Ghith, 'Exemption of Non-Performance of the Seller's Contractual Obligations' (2006) 20 (3) Arab Law Quarterly 270; T. Weitzmann, 'Validity and Excuse in the U.N. Sales' (1997) 16 Journal of Law and Commerce 285. Because the impediment is not defined in both Conventions, the national courts could pinpoint it through the lens of their municipal law. Thus, it is important to include the contract with a clarifying clause. Andreason (n 126) 356; Davies; Snyder (n 52) 327-332.

437Art. 79(2). Kröll et al (n 56) 1079.

438Ghith (n 435) 286.

439Shafiq (n 30) 257; Ghith (n 435) 287.

440Schwenzer, Commentary (n 52) 1079.

third party[441] for damages: this would cause unjust enrichment.[442] However, if the contract between the Egyptian company and the third party is under a domestic law that does not exempt the third party from paying indemnity, then the Egyptian company will gain damages. Thus, CISG should stipulate first that the impediment of the third party is unforeseeable and unavoidable to the original party and, second, that the third party is exempted, under the applicable law governing their relationship, from damages.

8. Conclusion

Disputes arising from the contravention of international commercial contracts should be settled pursuant to a uniform set of norms to provide international trade with legal clarity[443] and to ensure the proper standards for commercial contracts at the global level.[444] Multilateral agreements, like ULIS and CISG, urge a process of harmonisation towards achieving a unified international legal framework.[445] This paper has reviewed the differences between these Conventions[446] to determine which one best satisfies the needs of universal merchandising. It finds as a result of the comparison that the techniques employed in CISG surpass those of ULIS. For instance, unlike ULIS, CISG designates exactly[447] when

---

[441]Tires company.

[442]Shafiq (n 30) 258.

[443]Louis Marquis, International Uniform Commercial Law: Toward a Progressive Consciousness (Hampshire, Ashgate Publishing 2005) 101.

[444]Andreason (n 126) 355. Therefore, there will be greater flow of goods internationally, which fosters the notion of international marketability. Trakman, Ranieri (n 30) 480-493.

[445]Dalhuisen (n 14) 627-629.

[446]Franz Werro, 'Notes on the Purpose and Aims of Comparative Law' (2001) 75(4) Tulane Law Review 1226.

[447]ULIS Art. 19(2). Honnold, Documentary (n 62) 115; Tunc (n 62) 46.

delivery commitments should be made, i.e. handing over the goods to the first carrier.[448]

The comparability of the structural and functional elements of both Conventions facilitates the detection of their imperfections and aids scholars to make recommendations any novel changes in compliance with contemporary commerce standards. For example, parties are able to declare the contract terminated in the case of a fundamental breach without supervision from either the tribunal or the court,[449] and both Conventions strictly require a fundamental breach to terminate the contract. However, they are lenient on the issue of defining this breach.

This work shows that CISG in many cases resolves the systemic imperfections of ULIS in order to achieve harmonisation among states. Many provisions demonstrate the doctrine of CISG which is to reduce the application of the termination mechanism on international contracts, such as averting automatic avoidance.[450] CISG also offsets the interests of both parties on grounds of equity in many provisions.[451] For example, the court's period of grace is prohibited in relation to any of the parties' obligations,[452] contrary to ULIS, which permits granting such a period in case of the buyer's failure to take the delivery.[453] Further, CISG omits some of the requirements of ULIS, which are more suitable to national sales, such as the stipulation to invite the seller to examine the goods to demonstrate the existence of defects in order to claim non-con-

---

[448]Shafiq (n 30) 137; Schwenzer, Commentary (n 52) 929.

[449]E. Sleem, The international Sale (Alexandria, Monshaat Alma'ref 2004) 82.

[450]Schlechtriem (n 101) 176. ULIS departs from the CISG's jurisprudence, which considers avoidance as a last resort. Goode et al (n 13) 52; Bonell, 'The UNIDROIT Principles' (n 13) 286.

[451]CISG Art. 25. Will, M. 'General Provisions: Article 25', in Bianca; Bonell (n 16) 215.

[452]ULIS Art. 24(3).

[453]ULIS Art. 64. Bianca; Bonell (n 16) 443.

formity.[454] On the other hand, the sphere of application of ULIS is much wider than that of CISG. For instance, if the defects of the goods causes an explosion which damages the buyer's warehouse and causes mortal harm to one of the buyer's workers,[455] under ULIS the seller bears all losses incurred by the buyer, such as compensation for the detriment of other commodities, the loss of the profits if they were sold[456] and the compensation for the injured worker.[457] Corporal injuries are excluded under CISG.[458]

This evaluation of Conventions is beneficial to states as it allows them to make a more informed decision on which Convention to ratify or to use as a model law for their domestic statutes. It also assists the contracting parties to exclude provisions of one Convention from their contract[459] or adopt the perspective of another, as applicable. A comparative study reveals the need for statutory modification in some provisions, something that is incompatible with the norms of international trade practice.[460] For instance, some Articles in both Conventions are no longer relevant or applicable, such those associated with the place of payment because of the shift to electronic payment.[461] Furthermore, this comparison helps the parties to discover major gaps when an interpretation can be found neither in the convention's Articles nor in its general principles.[462] The parties should design their contract in the knowledge

---

[454]The second sentence of Article 39(2) of ULIS. Graveson et al (n 66) 76-77.

[455]Heuze (n 59) 402.

[456]CISG Art. 74 & ULIS Art. 82. M. Alsharqawi, International Commercial Contracts (Cairo, Dar Alnahda Alarabeya 2002) 209 -210.

[457]In cases where the seller predicted or ought to predict such consequence of their breach at the time of concluding the contract. ULIS Art. 82.

[458]CISG Art. 5.

[459]Mckendrick (n 17) [9].

[460]Werro (n 445) 1227.

[461]Mark Parry; Tomoko Kawakami, 'Virtual Word of Mouth and Willingness to Pay for Consumer Electronic Innovations' (2015) 32(2) Journal of Product Innovation Management 192.

[462]Bianca; Bonell (n 16) 66; Fawcett et al (n 15) 930-931.

of a Convention's gap, choosing to follow in these instances, for example the conduct of ULIS or to adopt the rules of other international instruments (e.g. UNIDROIT Principles[463] or International General Conditions such as the conditions issued by the European Economic Commission on the Supply of Machinery Equipment Contracts)[464] in their contractual terms. As the great number of national laws constitutes a stumbling block to the flow of international trade in goods, filling gaps in the terms of the contract is crucial to minimise the chance of domestic law being applied.[465] Consequently, the parties can confidently sign the contract and envisage that future conflicts will be solved either by the convention or by their contractual clauses.

More importantly, steps should be taken to create an International Commercial Court[466] to ultimately promote uniformity and attain internationality.[467] This aim of harmonisation helps actors across the world to act in a more fraternal way[468] being under the umbrella of one legal system that motivates the sharing and exchange of legal perspectives. In this way, dissolving the frontiers between states through a unified substantive law will move away from different legal families and help to transform the vast global civilization into a more international community.

---

[463]Bonell, An International Restatement of Contract Law: The UNIDROIT Principles of International Commercial Contracts (n 19) 305.

[464]Shafiq (n 30) 8-11.

[465]Magnus (n 18) 266-267; Mckendrick (n 17) [9].

[466]Michael Bridge, 'Issues Arising under Articles 64, 72 and 73 of the United Nations Convention on Contracts for the International Sale of Goods' (2006) 25 The Journal of Law and Commerce 405.

[467]CISG aims to promote uniformity. CISG Art. 7(1).

[468]Tunc (n 62) 2.

Legal Issues Journal 10(1) 2024: 9–82. ©The UK Law and Society Association

Differences between CISG and ULIS

Feature	CISG	ULIS
Delivery of the goods	The seller will fulfil their commitment of delivery if they hand the goods over to the first inland carrier *for transmission to the buyer*.	ULIS does not designate exactly which carrier the seller should hand the goods over to, to determine the passage of risk.
	CISG usually separates the obligation of delivery and the obligation of goods' conformity.	Obligation of delivery is not complete unless the goods conform to the contract.
Selling in transit	The risk passes to the second buyer at the time of concluding the second contract.	The risk passes to the second buyer retroactively from the time the goods were handed over to the carrier.
The obligation of confirming packaging of the goods	It is mentioned in detail.	It is not mentioned.
Sale by sample	Consignment of a sample is a guarantee of the quality of the purchased goods to be received unless it is agreed otherwise.	Consignment of a sample does not mean that the seller will provide similar goods.

Goods' ordinary purpose	CISG refers to ordinary purposes of the goods (plural) enabling the buyer to reject the goods if they are not suitable to fulfil one of their main purposes.	ULIS states that goods should be suitable for their ordinary use (singular), which means that the goods should match with only one of the main purposes.
Claim of third persons	CISG limits the seller's liability through specifying the relevant laws to determine whether or not the seller is in breach.	The law is not specified.
Time of assessing conformity	CISG only requires the defects to exist before risk is passed to the buyer in order for the seller to be blamed, regardless of who caused the defect.	ULIS protects the buyer's right to claim non-conformity when the defects occur before the delivery, and when such defects are the result of the seller's own actions (or their agent's).
Inspection of goods	CISG requires examination of the goods to take place in '… as short a period as is practicable in the circumstances'.	ULIS imposes on the buyer the responsibility of examining the goods 'promptly' once they are handed over.
Notice of conformity	The buyer should notify the seller within 'reasonable time' of any lack of conformity after examining the goods.	The buyer should notify the seller 'promptly' of any lack of conformity after examining the goods.

Specific performance used by the buyer	If a seller's breach of the contract occurs because the goods suffer from a lack of conformity, the buyer can ask for specific performance.	ULIS, unlike CISG, forbids the buyer from resorting to such a remedy if the buyer is reasonably able to purchase alternative goods.
Reduction of price	CISG confines this mechanism to the non-conformity of goods.	The buyer can use this remedy in response to a deficiency of any of the seller's obligations.
Price of payment	CISG does not state that payment and delivery are concurrent conditions, because this corresponds to internal sale.	ULIS states that payment and delivery are concurrent conditions.
Buyer facilitating delivery	Buyers should carry out all actions that are 'reasonably expected' to facilitate delivery.	The buyer should undertake everything that is 'necessary' to enable the seller to hand over the goods.
Taking over the goods	The buyer should take over the goods, but CISG does not stipulate 'actual take' to be compatible with the practice in international trade.	ULIS imposes on the buyer the responsibility of 'actually' taking the goods over.

Specific performance used by the seller	If the buyer has not performed any of their obligations, such as paying the purchase price or taking the delivery, the seller may turn to the court to ask for specific performance.	ULIS stipulates two restrictions: (i) this mechanism is restricted to non-payment of price; and (ii) the seller is not entitled to require the buyer to pay the price when it is reasonably possible for them to resell the goods.
Avoiding the contract due to the buyer's breach of paying the price	the seller can declare the contract avoided.	The seller should either ask the buyer to pay the price or declare the contract avoided. This decision should occur within a reasonable time, otherwise the contract will be *automatically avoided*.
Designating the specifications of goods	CISG only permits the seller to decide on the goods' specifications, but does not allow them to avoid the contract on the basis of the buyer's failure to designate such specifications.	The seller may either determine the specification themselves or declare avoidance directly after the buyer's failure to determine the goods' specifications.
Anticipatory breach	CISG broadens incidents for Anticipatory breach to include: (i) acute deficiency in creditworthiness; (ii) serious deficiency in ability to perform; and (iii) a party's conduct in performing the contract.	Such suspension cannot be utilised unless the counterparty is confronting a difficult economic situation, such as the buyer being declared bankrupt.

Instalment contract	If a party commits a fundamental breach in relation to one delivery, or instalment, the other party may declare avoidance merely in respect to that instalment.	ULIS does not address the partial avoidance.
Damages	CISG specifies the current value by referring to the place where the goods were agreed to be delivered to the buyer.	The current value would be based on the market of the place in which the transaction occurs.

Legal Issues Journal 10(1) 2024: 83–103. ©The UK Law and Society Association

The current status of compensation, support, and resettlement when the State acquires land for socio-economic development purposes[1]

Cao Thanh Son[2]

Mechanisms and policies for compensation, support, and resettlement when the State acquires land for socio-economic development purposes are concretized by the 2013 Land Law, aiming to harmonize the interests of the parties. However, the report from the General Department of Land Management (in 2018) said that the adjusted documents on compensation and support have yet to cover all the problems arising in practice, leading to difficulties and confusion in implementation (Nhan, 2022).In essence, the land acquisition is within the competence of the State; in contrast to the types of assets established on the land, there must be a voluntary mechanism of agreement. In this case, the State should not use its power to impose compensation prices. Although the purpose is to acquire land for economic development, the law empowers the State to decide on the value of land assets, and set on the land is not standard. When comparing the same type of asset, but the value

---

[1]This research is funded by University of Economics and Law, Vietnam National University Ho Chi Minh, Vietnam.
[2]Ph.D. Candidate, University of Economics and Law, Ho Chi Minh City, Vietnam and Vietnam National University, Ho Chi Minh, Vietnam. Email: caothanhsonagjustice@gmail.com. https://orcid.org/0009-0007-0540-3801.

Legal Issues Journal 10(1) 2024: 83–103. ©The UK Law and Society Association

of each place has a difference, there is no uniformity. In many localities, the market price has changed several times but still set meager compensation prices for people.From the above issue, when conducting compensation when the State acquires land for socio-economic development purposes, in any case, it is necessary to correctly and fully calculate the damage caused by land acquisition to the subjects who are using land and assets attached to land, including related intangible and tangible damage. In addition, it is also necessary to delete the support policy because when the damage is fully estimated, there is no need for support-related regulations

Keywords: Land acquisition, economic development, compensation, support, and resettlement.

Introduction

Under Article 54 of the 2013 Constitution, only in case of extreme necessity, the State shall acquire land from land users for socio-economic development in the national and public interests as prescribed by law. When land acquisition is inevitable, the method of implementation, as well as the determination of damage, should be considered carefully, absolutely not abusing power to deprive people of their lawful property. To do this, the corresponding legal grounds must meet the actual requirements set out. However, the provisions of the law on compensation, support, and resettlement upon land acquisition for socio-economic development still contain many inadequacies that need to be improved.

1. Methodology

To clarify the research problems, the author uses the methodology of dialectical materialism and historical materialism of Marxism-Leninism to study the problem in the State of movement, constant change and place in the overall relationship, and the interaction between the phenomenon to be studied with other phenomena. Moreover, the subject of study is considered and evaluated in the State of "moving...", making the research problem rich, diverse, traditional, and modern.

In addition, the author also applies the following research methodologies:

Doctrinal legal research methodology: This method is applied by the author to understand doctrines and theories directly related to the research topic, from which to build a solid foundation in building a theoretical framework for the research problem.

Analytical legal research methodology: The method is applied to clarify regulations related to land acquisition, specifically analyzing legal provisions related to land acquisition, determining the purpose of land acquisition, balancing and regulating interests between subjects when the land acquisition process takes place, thereby pointing out the inadequacies and limitations from a legislative perspective within the scope of the research topic.

Statistical methodology: This method is applied by the author to collect statistics and synthesize essential data directly related to the research scope of the topic, e.g., statistics related to the level of satisfaction of people whose land is acquired regarding compensation land prices, life and production support mechanisms, the data on complaints and lawsuits related to the compensation, support, and resettlement mechanism.

Comparative legal research methodology: The author applies it when there is a comparison of the advantages and disadvantages of legal provisions between the laws of Vietnam and some countries in the world, thereby having the most objective view when providing timely solutions to problems that have been set out in the scope of the research topic.

2. The Findings and Discussion

In the legal aspect, based on the concept of land acquisition, the interpretation of the concept of land acquisition for socio-economic development in the national and public interests is as follows:

> "Land acquisition for socio-economic development in the national and public interests is the State's decision to acquire the land use rights of persons who are granted land use rights by the State or acquire land of land users who violate the land law to serve the needs of socio-economic development based on maintaining a peaceful and stable environment for the implementation of national industrialization and modernization along the socialist orientation, ensuring that all people and society enjoy the land values brought about after the acquisition."

Many research opinions believe that "Land acquisition for socio-economic development for national and public benefits" needs to have its "intent" clarified. In the long term, it is necessary to replace the term "The State acquires land for socio-economic development" with "The State acquires land use rights." In essence, this will help change perspectives towards an increasingly progressive society. Accordingly, "Towards unification between the Constitution and the Land Law, it is necessary to limit the State's authority to acquire land to cases where it is necessary to use the land to serve national interests, public interests, and national defense and security interests" (Vo, 2013,p.11). Also, Son (2018),s argues that because some projects bring benefits to businesses, but in order to reduce compensation costs, they often take advantage of gaps in regulations and assign State land acquisition mechanisms. In this case, there is no harmony between the interests of the State, the interests of investors, and the people whose land is acquired. The lack of transparency is a premise for violations by state management agencies in the land.

3 Compensation, support, and resettlement when the State acquires land for socio-economic development purposes

3.1 Compensation when the State acquires land for socio-economic development purposes

According to nationwide statistics, 63/63 provinces and centrally-run cities have issued specific regulations on compensation, support, and resettlement levels according to the decentralization of the Land Law and Government Decrees to be applied locally. In particular, regulations clearly define the responsibilities of departments, agencies, units, and organizations involved in implementing compensation, support, and resettlement. However, when considering the compensation mechanism, many things could be more consistent. Specifically, regarding compensation for moving costs when the State acquires land for socio-economic development purposes, in different localities, there is no uniformity in regulations e.g. there are 7/63 regulated provinces and cities compensated for travel expenses divided by distance; 6/63 provinces and cities compensated according to actual costs; by house type or house construction area acquired (8/63 provinces); according to administrative units at commune, district, and province levels from 2,000,000 VND to 15,000,000 VND (32/63 provinces); There is no regulation on compensation for travel expenses (10/63 provinces) (Nhan, 2022) In general, according to Hien and Thang (2021), land valuation to have a basis for calculating compensation for land is a susceptible category because conflicts of interest may arise. Based on clause 3, Article 112 of the 2013 Land Law, the State acquires land for socio-economic development, and the land price calculated for compensation "must be consistent with the prevailing land price on the market." It is also imposing, as determining specific land prices tends to be lower than the market price (Thai, 2016, p.11). "Maybe it is only relative because the market price has many fluctuations" (Hien, 2017, p.98-99). The determination of compensation value is based only on the current land use status, not considering the increase in land value after the State acquires land from people and investors implementing the project. The State's land price frame is only about 20% - 30% of the market land price frame. The provincial land price range is only 30% - 60% of the local market land price. It leads to a situation where when land is acquired, the compensation land price is far lower than the market price (Huyen & Ha, 2022, p.165). Recognizing the process of land allocation to implement investment projects in Da Nang, with land areas A2 and A3 belonging to the Son Tra-Dien Ngoc Resettlement Area project in Da Nang City decided the compensation unit price of 2,570,000 VND/m2 for affected households, the total compensation amount for parcel A2 is 25 billion VND and area A3 is 63 billion VND, respectively (Than, 2020). After one month from the date the Da Nang People's Committee allocated the land, the enterprise transferred the project to the new investor. Accordingly, the value of parcel A2 is 133 billion VND, a difference of 107 billion VND compared to the original unit price.[3]

Through consultation, the research sample includes 540 households whose land was acquired for socio-economic development purposes in 2020, of which 188 households in Ha Noi and Ho Chi Minh City 177 households, City. Da Nang 175 households. The questionnaire uses a Likert scale (5-point scale). Research results show that the level of people's satisfaction with compensation and support when the State acquires land for economic development and community service purposes is generally low at 2.54 points; People's perception of land compensation price is 2.32 points; The change in life after the State acquired land compared to expectations, was not rated highly with 2.45 points (Phuong, 2021).In a situation of economic development, the exercise of the right to re-

---

[3]Notice of Inspection Conclusion No. 160/TBKL-TTCP dated January 17, 2013, of the Government Inspectorate on the responsibilities of Da Nang City People's Committee in complying with the law on inspection, complaints, and denunciations of corruption, inspection of some investment projects using land, p. 5

claim land has the potential to create surplus value that only profits belong to the final owner of the property, not the original owner. Suppose the surplus is greater than the cost of land acquisition. In that case, it means that the organization that is transferred land use rights will gain a surplus, which gives them an incentive to persuade the government to carry out land acquisition on their behalf even when the land area acquired is only for personal gain. Therefore, laws in developed countries such as the UK and the US will require courts to carefully consider when using the right to compulsory land requisition to serve the public interest when **"one or a few people will capture the surplus value"** (Gallagher, 2005, p.77)

Explaining the reason why compensation land prices have not approached market prices some scholars give many reasons. In particular, the time to determine the specific land price has yet to be clarified, as Clause 2, Article 74 of the 2013 Land Law stipulates that the Provincial People's Committee decides the specific land price at the time of land acquisition decision. However, there is still no document guiding "when to decide on land acquisition (Hien, 2017, p.98-99) When comparing experience in India under Article 22, Part 3 of the Land Acquisition Act, in case land is needed for economic development, the State calculates compensation according to the market value of the land; land damage will be considered to decide the compensation level at the time of land acquisition notification. In addition to the market price basis, the Court may consider adding 30% of the compensation value because this is a case of compulsory land acquisition (Ministry of Natural Resources and Environment, 2012, p.19) According to experience from Australia in Article 55 of the WA Land Management Act 1997, compensation for land is determined according to the principle of "value to the owner," recognizing that the compensation level is higher than the market value. Value to the owner includes the market value of the affected interest, exceptional value due to the ownership or use of the acquired land, damage due to the land parcel being divided, noise damage, or other damage. The price for calculating compensation is the current market price, decided with the management agency in consultation with the head of the valuation agency.

According to the Ministry of Natural Resources and Environment (2012, p.19-20), market value is determined as the amount of money that the asset can be sold voluntarily and readily at a specific time. In addition Hien (2017, p.98-99) citing Section 5 (2) Land Compensation Act 1961 Clause 2 Article 5 Law on Compensation for Land Damage 1961 of the United Kingdom avers that in some developed countries, the Valuation date is the "legally fixed date" to determine all assets according to the market return on that date.

Referring to the problem and experience in Taiwan under Taiwan's Land Occupation Law in 2000, real estate valuation needs to distinguish between the value of land and assets created on land. The compensation price for land is the value at the time of land allocation; the compensation value for construction works on land is calculated according to the price of replacement works with equivalent conditions (Vo, 2012). Thereby, the compensation price for land is for public benefit purposes, and some countries have compensation calculations higher than the market price. Because, after all, this is a compulsory land-acquiring mechanism, which may be contrary to the wishes of land users. Unlike British law and some developed countries, our country's law does not widely recognize cases of compensation for damages that occur even though land is not acquired (Hien, 2018). Because when determining compensation, our country defines the scope "according to the law." Unforeseen arising damages will be outside the scope. In addition, Vietnam's prediction mechanism only limits damage during the land acquisition process, with invisible damage, damage from the time of land acquisition notice (before land acquisition), or damage after the land acquisition process has not been calculated.

Regulations on the mechanism for seizing land for public purposes, annual land valuation, and adjusting land prices to calculate compensation in Taiwan have many similarities with Vietnam. The fundamental difference is that the agency with authority to decide land prices and compensation values belongs to the valuation committee, consisting of many members, and is not decided by an administrative agency like in Vietnam. Notably, at the provincial level, there is a specialized management agency for land prices, assisting local leaders independent of the financial management agency and land management agency. Vietnam can consider Taiwan's experience to apply a mechanism that assigns responsibility for deciding land prices according to the market and compensation levels to a land valuation committee. The law can assign many different tasks related to land prices to this committee, such as resolving land price disputes and resolving land price complaints (Vo, 2012).

3.2 Support when the State acquires land for socio-economic development purposes

The 2013 Land Law in Clause 14, Article 3 states:

> Support when the State acquires land is the State's assistance to people whose land is acquired, to stabilize their lives, production and development.

Support amounts are understood as the added value when the State reviews compensation payments; this is a regulation from the added value of land, not brought by the investment of the land user.

There are three primary forms of support when the State acquires land for socio-economic development purposes:

> Regarding support for training, career change, and job search when the State acquires land for socio-economic development purposes

Support policies represent the vision of the State because the land acquisition process can disrupt people's lives, and providing support helps minimize the social problems that arise. Accordingly, the Prime Minister issued Decision 63/2015/QD-TTg related to vocational training policies and job creation for workers after the land acquisition process took place, institutionalizing regulations in localities have also issued documents guiding relevant content such as Decision 24/2017/QD-UBND of the Ha Noi People's Committee on supporting vocational training and job search, or implementation plans. Decision 63/2015/QD-TTg in Ho Chi Minh City (Huyen, 2022, p.38), or Decision No. 08/2015/QD-UBND dated March 24, 2015, of Nam Dinh Provincial People's Committee regulating unit prices for vocational training and job search support. However, the support mechanism when the State acquires land for socio-economic development purposes needs to clarify the following issues:

Firstly, the form of support for training, career change, and job search does not stipulate the minimum land area to be acquired. It leads to acquiring only a few square meters of Agricultural land, still enjoying the policy. Logically, it is necessary to reconsider because, in reality, people will not lose their jobs at all.

Secondly, Point a, Clause 1, Article 20 of Decree 47/2014/ND-CP stipulates:

> Monetary support is not more than 05 times the price of agricultural land of the same type in the local land price list for the entire area of agricultural land acquired, the supported area does not exceed the local agricultural land allocation limit." Agricultural land is acquired, the supported area does not exceed the local agricultural land allocation limit.

The law only specifies a maximum support limit of no more than five times the price of agricultural land but does not indicate a minimum limit. It may lead to differential support between localities (Hien & Thang, 2014, p.389-390).

Thirdly, according to Hien (2019) land is a means of production, but the nature of the support sometimes does not help people whose land is acquired to reestablish their livelihoods. Because there is no data to orient the use of compensation and support accordingly, statistics in the southern provinces have about 57.5% of people using the amount of compensation and support for the construction of new houses, 8.72% buying utensils and living. At that time, only 2.55% of people used the compensation money to support career change and finding new jobs. Therefore, after only a few years of spending all the supported money, with no means of production left, the people whose land was acquired fell into poverty (Minh, 2010, p.g5)

3.3. Support to stabilize life and production when the State acquires land for socio-economic development purposes

Compared to the past, the 2013 Land Law has clearly defined the conditions and beneficiaries of policies related to support when the State recovers land as households and individuals directly engaged in agricultural production. Accordingly, in Clause 3, Article 19 of Decree 47/2014 / ND-CP, the support for life stabilization is as follows:

a) Acquire from 30% to 70% of the currently used agricultural land area, receive support for six months in case of not relocating, and 12 months in case of having to relocate. If moving to areas with challenging socio-economic conditions, the maximum support period is 24 months.

In cases where more than 70% of the agricultural land area in use is acquired, support will be provided for 12 months if there is no need to relocate and for 24 months if there is a period of relocation; in cases of having to move to areas with difficult socio-economic conditions or poor socio-economic conditions.

b) The prescribed land acquisition area is determined according to each land acquisition decision of the competent People's Committee. For challenging situations, the maximum support period is 36 months;

From the regulations on conditions to determine the amount of life support when the State acquires agricultural land, the following observations can be drawn:

Firstly, Decree 47/2014/ND-CP defines many limits on land to be acquired to ensure fairness for land users. However, this change is only partially comprehensive and meets social requirements. Because a household may have a small amount of land acquired but still benefits from the support policy (for example, losing 100m2/200m2 will be converted to 50% of existing agricultural land). On the contrary, subjects whose land area to be acquired is many times larger may not be considered for support (for example, losing 3,000m2/20,000m2 currently); this shows that there will be a case of losing a large land area, but The percentage conversion on the existing land area is relatively small. Therefore, this issue needs to be considered and corrected promptly.

Secondly, as noted in Hien (2021), the regulations to support life stabilization are determined according to each acquisition decision, showing that there will be cases affected by many different acquisition decisions. However, with each decision to acquire lost land Fragmented, although we know that the total lost land area is quite large, each decision will need more support consideration ratio.

Thirdly, the assistance was calculated at the price of rice, which was then converted into money, which proved illogical. If this is determined from the beginning according to the regional minimum wage, it will appear reasonable and fair between subjects when rice prices have specific differences (Vo, 2015). Phuong (2019), argues that essentially, a **"stable life" must** contain the most comprehensive values such as food, accommodation, travel, entertainment, and so on. The valuation of rice does not represent the core of its nature.

3.4 Resettlement when the State acquires land for socio-economic development purposes

Land acquisition/expropriation, forcible evictions, forcible displacement of people from their homes for development projects, and business projects (roads, plants, hydropower, industrial parks, urban areas, and others) occur in many countries. Eviction risks harming the right to housing and many other social rights (education, health care, employment) of the population.[4] The seriousness of forced evictions from the place of residence has long been of concern to the international community. In 1976, the United Nations Conference on Settlements noted that countries must pay special attention to eviction and that "eviction activities are carried out only when conservation and restoration are not possible, and resettlement measures have been taken."

Practical application related to the level of resettlement support in Vietnam shows that the level of support can be in money or equal to the value of infrastructure investment in concentrated resettlement (45/63 provinces). There is support from 5% to 50% of land compensation value (7/63 provinces); Support based on a percentage (%) of the value of the minimum resettlement rate (6/63 provinces)... three provinces do not stipulate this support (Nghe An, Da Nang, and Long An), regarding the minimum resettlement rate, including regulations: minimum resettlement rate equal to residential land; minimum resettlement rate equal to housing; minimum resettlement rate in cash.

There are 53/63 provinces and centrally-run cities that regulate the minimum resettlement rate equal to residential land, with different areas depending on the conditions of each locality... ten

---

[4]Office of the United Nations High Commissioner for Human Rights, Forced evictions and human rights: https://www.ohchr.org/EN/Issues/LandAndHR/Pages/ForcedEvictions.aspx, excerpted from La La Khanh Tung, "Land acquisition: international human rights standards and some issues in Vietnam," Conference proceedings: Theoretical and practical basis of amending the Land Law in 2013, National University Ha Noi, November 24, 2021, page 221.

provinces do not regulate this content. There are 27/63 provinces and centrally-run cities that stipulate the minimum resettlement rate is equal to apartment buildings with different minimum areas or according to the resettlement housing area of the approved project... 36/63 provinces do not stipulate a minimum resettlement rate equal to housing (Nhan, 2022).

The minimum resettlement rate in money is regulated in localities according to each administrative unit of commune, ward, and town (ranging from 25 to 300 million VND) or according to the minimum resettlement area multiplied by the land price. Expressly, at the resettlement location or the average investment value for each resettlement rate, 16 provinces do not stipulate a minimum resettlement rate in money.

Resettlement arrangements in localities are carried out by allocating residential land or houses with a total residential land area for resettlement of 567.40 hectares for 25,770 households and individuals (an average of 220.18 m2/household) and the house area for resettlement is 29,745 m2 for 347 households and individuals deployed in Quang Ninh province. For households and individuals who care for their accommodation, the State will support them with money to find accommodation and resettlement in the amount of 1,218 million VND. Localities generally carry out resettlement using residential land, and resettlement housing areas are mainly carried out in cities with limited residential land funds (Nhan, 2022).

Based on Article 86 of the 2013 Land Law, inheriting and supplementing the principles of resettlement in case of land acquisition that requires relocation as follows: (i) The resettlement plan must be made public; (ii) People whose land is acquired will be given priority for on-site resettlement if there is a resettlement project or resettlement conditions in the land acquisition area; (iii) Prioritize convenient locations for people whose land is acquired to hand over the site early; (iv) Priority will be given to those whose land is acquired and who have contributed to the revolution: (v) Receive enough financial support from the State to buy a minimum resettlement rate if compensation is lacking, support if not enough to buy a minimum resettlement rate. In this case, the land use fee calculation will be based on the specific land price at the resettlement place, and the Provincial People's Committee will decide the selling price of the house in the resettlement place. However, central legal documents need to mention the issue of guidance on determining land prices and land use fees that people must pay when receiving resettlement grounds. Based on research from local documents. In addition, Clause 4, Article 86 of the 2013 Land Law stipulates: "If compensation and support money are not enough to buy a minimum resettlement rate, the State will support money enough to buy a minimum resettlement rate." However, with Clause 1, Article 22 of Decree 47/2014/ND-CP, this issue is stipulated as follows: "Vietnamese households and individuals residing abroad receive residential land and houses. Resettlement, where the amount of compensation for land is less than the value of a minimum resettlement rate, will be subsidized by the difference between the value of the minimum resettlement rate and the amount of compensation for land. From the above issue, it can be seen that the conditions for support in the two regulations mentioned above are contradictory; if the Land Law is based on calculating total compensation and support (compensation for land, assets attached to land, and other supports, if any), the Decree only considers calculating compensation related to land (Hien & Trang, 2013). In addition, the time for handing over residential land and houses is determined based on Clause 3, Article 85 of the 2013 Land Law, which stipulates: "Residential land acquisition will only be carried out after completing the construction of housing or infrastructure of the resettlement area." In general, the completion of construction is different from the resettled people who will be handed over land and resettlement houses soon. Through the study, the authors found that there still need to be documents specifying the time of handing over land and resettlement houses (Than, 2017).

Besides, there is still no close attention related to the post-resettlement process; the case of resettlement in Ha Noi is a typical example when 173 resettlement apartment buildings were handed over. At that time, there were 103 buildings without community houses, only 119 buildings with service business areas, and 54 buildings without parking spaces; the number of established management boards needed to be more significant. According to the data reported by Ha Noi Housing Management and Development Company, by the end of 2018, out of more than 100 resettlement apartment projects, there were over 700 resettlement apartments for ground clearance. However, people have yet to come to carry out procedures for handover, and the number of vacant apartments accounts for a relatively large proportion, with more than 370 apartments[5]. Therefore, it is necessary to set up management boards in resettlement areas to receive and handle relevant issues in the resettlement area.

In addition, the 2013 Land Law does not stipulate a "policy for dealing with temporary accommodation (temporary residence)." However, it can be understood as still containing "policy for dealing with temporary accommodation (temporary residence)." However, this leads to the understanding of some localities that do not regulate "policy for dealing with temporary accommodation (temporary residence)." Clause 3, Article 6 of the 2014 Housing Law on resettlement housing arrangement stipulates: "In case the State invests in renovating or rebuilding an apartment building, the project investor must provide temporary accommodation or pay for resettled people to take care of their accommodation during the renovation and reconstruction period; In case a real estate business and the owner agree to invest in renovating and rebuilding an apartment building, the parties shall agree on the temporary accommodation of the owner during the renovation and rebuilding

---

[5]Central Management Board of Irrigation Projects (CPO): Resettlement Policy Framework (RPF), Ha Noi, June 2013 http://agrovi- et.g-vo.vn/Lists/appsp01_Jawdocumenlist/Attachments/111/KhungCS_-TaiDC.pdf, dated February 26, 2019

period." Proposal to amend and supplement clause 2, Article 83 of the Land Law with the content: "Support for temporary accommodation (temporary residence) for cases where households, individuals, and Vietnamese residing abroad have to relocate." in order to ensure the consistency of the legal system, making it easy for localities to implement and satisfactorily address people's temporary residence needs while waiting for resettlement (Dang, 2021).s

4. CONCLUSION

In the process of national economic development, land acquisition is an inevitable and objective issue, serving the common goal of socio-economic development. Although, the law on land acquisition has changed many times from time to time in order to suit the social context. However, there still exist "gaps" in legal provisions when the issue of regulating the harmonious balance between the interests of subjects such as the State, investors, and people whose land is recovered in the process of compulsory land transfer and use of land for socio-economic development objectives has not yet been addressed.

Accordingly, the compensation, support, and resettlement when the State recovers land for socio-economic development should be built on the following theoretical foundations: (i) towards the management and coordination of land in a scientific manner, helpful for life, society and people, (ii) towards ensuring fairness and equality in the process of the State conducting compensation, support and resettlement when recovering a land area, (iii) to heighten the responsibility of the State, the relevant subjects in the process of land recovery, towards the goal of sustainable development.

Legal Issues Journal 10(1) 2024: 83–103. ©The UK Law and Society Association

References

Clause 1 Article 5 Decision 60/2017/QD-UBND of Ho Chi Minh City People's Committee

Conference proceedings: Assessing some limitations in implementing the 2013 Land Law and proposing solutions," Vietnam Union of Science and Technology Associations, pp. 85-90

Dang, K. 2021. Amending and supplementing the 2013 Land Law - Recommendations and proposals from Ho Chi Minh City. Natural Resources and Environment Magazine, 17: 9-13.

Decision 03/2018/QD-UBND dated January 30, 2018, of Dong Nai Provincial People's Committee.

Gallagher, E.F. 2005. Breaking New Ground: Using Eminent Domain for Economic Development. Fordham L. Rev, 73(1837). Retrieved from https://ir.lawnet.fordham.edu/flr/vol73/iss4/13 .

Hien, P.T. 2019. The right to access information in land acquisition, compensation, support, and resettlement - viewed from the reality of Can Tho City. Legislative Studies Journal, 23: 49-50.

Hien, P.T. 2021. Things to know about compensation, support, and resettlement when the State acquires land. National Political Publishing House: 265.

Hien, P.T. & Thang, N.D. 2021. Ensuring the balance of interests between the State and people in determining a land price for compensation. Journal of Legal Studies, 6: 17.

Hien, P.T. & Trang, N.T.D. 2013. Solutions to enforce legal regulations on resettlement when the State acquires land. Can Tho University Journal of Science, 26: 75 -82.

Hien, P.T. & Vo Van Thang, V.V. 2014. Compensation, support, resettlement - results from a survey of households whose land was acquired in Can Tho city. Volume: The role of higher education in socio-economic development (Monograph): 389-390.

Hien, P.T. 2017. Determining land prices to calculate compensation when the state acquires land. Legislative Studies Journal, 1+2/2017: 98-99.

Hien, P.T. 2018. Legislation on compensation and site clearance in Vietnam - Balancing the interests between the State and the People's interests. Can Tho University Journal of Science, 10: 114.

Hien, P.T. 2018. Things to know about compensation, support, and resettlement when the State acquires land. National Political Publishing House: 127.

Huyen , H.K. & Ha, N. T. N. 2022. Causes of failure of the policy mechanism to regulate land added value in Vietnam. Proceedings of the national scientific conference Resolution 18/NQ-TU/2022 and issues raised in amending the 2013 Land Law, National Economics University. Ha Noi, National Economics University Publishing House: 165.

Huyen, L.T.N. 2022. Law on protecting the rights of land users when the State acquires land. Legal Profession Review, 5: 38.

Minh, P. 2010. Some solutions to create jobs for rural workers today. Agricultural Management Magazine, 170: 45.

Ministry of Natural Resources and Environment. 2012, September. Foreign experience on land management and law.

Nam, P.P. & Hanh, B. N. 2021. Policy to ensure "the plowman must have a field" in the conditions of using high-tech agricultural land. Natural Resources and Environment Magazine, 17:15.

Nhan, N.D. 2022. Looking back on ten years of implementing Resolution 19-NQ/TW: Current status of land acquisition, compensation, support, and resettlement. Retrieved June 20, 2022 from, https://baotainguyenmoitruong.vn/nhin-lai-10-nam-thuc-hien-nghi-quyet-19-nq-tw-bai-2-thuc-trang-cong-tac-thu-hoi-dat-boi-thuong-ho-tro-va-tai-dinh-cu-333906.html .

Nhan, N.D. 2022. Looking back on ten years of implementing Resolution 19-NQ/TW: Article No. 3: What are the cases where it is "extreme necessity" to acquire land?. Retrieved December 1, 2021, from, https://baotainguyenmoitruong.vn/nhin-lai-10-nam-thuc-hien-nghi-quyet-19-nq-tw-bai-3-dau-la-truong-hop-that-can-thiet-phai-thu-hoi-dat-334205.html .

Phuong, D.N. 2021. People's satisfaction in compensation and support when the State acquires land. Economy and Forecast Review, 12: 105-108.

Phuong, N.T. Improving the law on resettlement when the State acquires residential land, Journal of Education and Society, Vol. August: 78-82.

Phuong, N.T. 2019. Legislation on supporting life stabilization when the state acquires agricultural land and some recommendations for improvement.   Democracy and Law Review, 11(332): 42-47.

Phuong, N.T. 2020. Improve the law on support for training, career change, and job search when the State acquires agricultural land. State and Law Review, 7(387): 43-45.

Section 5 (2) Land Compensation Act 1961 (Clause 2 Article 5 Land Compensation Act 1961 of the United Kingdom)

Son, C. T. 2018. Land acquisition for socio-economic development for national and public benefits: Current situation and recommendations for amendments. Vietnam Trade and Industry Review, 12: 48.

Thai, L. Q. 2016. Legal issues about Vietnam's land use rights market. Hong Duc Publishing House: 36.

Than, C.H. 2017. Proposal to improve the 2013 Land Law. State and Law Review, 10: 79.

Than, C.H. 2020. Improving legal regulations on determining specific land prices. Legislative Studies Journal, 2(412): 28-31.

Tung, L.K. 2021. Land acquisition: international human rights standards and some issues in Vietnam. Conference proceedings: Theoretical and practical basis of amending the 2013 Land Law. Hanoi: Vietnam National University: 221.

Vo, D.H. (2013). Amending the Land Law needs a long-term vision and ensuring systematicity. Economy and Forecast Review, 7: 11.

Legal Issues Journal 10(1) 2024: 83–103. ©The UK Law and Society Association

Vo, D.H. 2012. International experience on land price management. Retrieved January 1, 2021, from https://tapchitaichin-
h.vn/nghien-cuu--trao-doi/trao-doi-binh-luan/kinh-nghiem-
quoc-te-ve-quan-ly-gia-dat-20380.html ..

Vo, P.V. 2015. The issue of support when the State acquires land in
the 2013 Land Law. Journal of Legal Studies. 1: 63.

Legal Issues Journal 10(1) 2024: 105-116. ©The UK Law and Society Association

Book Review: *Research Handbook on Intellectual Property and Artificial Intelligence*

Review by Alex Matheson[1]

Ryan Abbott, editor. *Research Handbook on Intellectual Property and Artificial Intelligence*. Research Handbooks in Intellectual Property series. Edward Elgar Publishing, 2022. ISBN: 978-1-80088-189-1.

Practical aspects of the book

This book is organised in four parts across 460 pages with extensive footnotes. It is helpfully indexed. The first part is multi-subject, and the others deal with different themes of intellectual property law. A range of technologies and jurisdictions are discussed across the chapters. Each part has an average of six chapters, with each chapter comprising an extensive article by one or more authors on an aspect of the interface between intellectual property law and artificial intelligence.

This formation and organisation of the book means that the work has the benefit of covering a broad range of ideas, representing the latest thinking from a wide range of perspectives and from a range

[1]DPhil (Candidate, Oxford University), Executive MBA (London Business School), LLM, MA, LLB (Hons); Barrister (England and Wales), Solicitor (Higher Rights, England and Wales); Software Engineer. Corresponding author: alex.matheson@sant.ox.ac.uk.

of jurisdictions. There can, of course, be no unifying theme nor central principle arising from overlaps between intellectual property law and artificial intelligence, nor is there any single intersection. There can be no single method of analysis. The book epitomises the fact that intellectual property law embodies different legal instruments, cases and principles in different jurisdictions, and artificial intelligence is a fluid field which encompasses different technologies in different contexts and at different times. Although different chapters deal with different aspects of these areas, each chapter is clear about its scope and the editor has done an impressive job of organising the book so that order is achieved. This is despite the fact that a reader is less likely to read the work from cover to cover, and more likely to 'dip in' to chapters of relevance to a given research topic.

Whilst since the book was published in 2022, there has been much technological innovation and much has been written about AI and intellectual property, the main ideas and principles of the book have lasted through these changes — as far as this reviewer can tell — and they will likely last through many future technological and legal changes.

Chapter selection for this review

Of the book, Chapters 7, 9, 13 (on copyright, within Part II) and chapter 14 (on trademarks, within part III) are covered in this review. These give a flavour of the overall work.

The AI-copyright challenge: tech neutrality, authorship, and the public interest

Examining first Chapter 7 'The AI-copyright challenge: tech neutrality, authorship, and the public interest', by Carys J. Craig. In this chapter, Craig explains that AI must be understood in the context of conventional constructs of copyright law, but notes that concepts such as 'original work of authorship' and 'non-obvious invention' look less solid in the context of modern technology and the unfolding AI-copyright drama (p.134).

Craig in this chapter is focusing primarily on the outputs of AI (p.134). After a useful and thorough discussion of background matters, technology neutrality and the purpose of copyright, Craig considers the AI challenge specifically and discusses the fact that a copyright drama also exists for AI inputs (from p.141).

Craig's extensive analysis appears to be as applicable to the AI of 2024 (today at the time of this review) as it was to the AI systems that existed at the time the chapter was written – likely to have been around 2020 from the technology discussed. Generative Pre-trained Transformers (GPTs) form the dominant AI technology at the time of this review and this type of technology is touched upon by Craig (see e.g., footnote 30—which discusses Open-AI's, then dominant, GPT-2).

Craig acknowledged at the time of writing the chapter that AI outputs lacked the aesthetic quality and conceptual coherence of human works (p.144), and the inference is made that the relationship between AI and copyright law depends, in part, on the quality of AI outputs. Craig's analysis here seems to be becoming more important over time, since as technology progresses, the quality of outputs is improving.

AI outputs remain the chapter's focus right up till near the end where issues relating to training data are re-introduced (p.152). Here, Craig highlights that 'copyright is, of course, premised on the exclusive right to make copies' and highlights that one implication of this is that we should be alert that this fact could unduly impede technological development—which gives rise to a policy dilemma since AI systems need to be trained on large corpuses of data (p.152).

As a potential solution to the problem that AI is not compatible with a strict interpretation of traditional copyright law, Craig proposes interpreting the law in light of the notion that copyright law's purpose is 'fundamentally expressive' (p.152). To make the case,

Craig notes that works of authorship are the result of a communicative act that is aimed at triggering a human response in the realm of emotions or cognition. This, Craig argues, is what is being protected. From this starting point, one can distinguish most AI systems as being purely functional and not human in their responses to communicative expression (p.153). Craig goes on, as others do (see below), to outline that much of the policy debate in relation to AI and copyright law concerns a fair use (or fair dealing) defence, and argues that most machine-learning training purposes, if not all, should be recognised as fair. (Contrast chapter 13, discussed below, which suggests that this is a US-centric view). Craig grants that it would be extremely cumbersome to carry out an assessment for each machine-learning training purpose to confirm that 'fair use' is established but suggests that a specific text and data mining exemption should apply (more on the limits of this UK concept appear in Chapter 13, discussed below). One reason for creating such an exemption (presumably in US law) would be in recognition of AI's potential contribution to a lively and rich public domain (p.155).

Copyright law should stay true to itself in the age of artificial intelligence

Chapter 9 (from p.179), 'Copyright law should stay true to itself in the age of artificial intelligence' by Alice Lee and Phoebe Woo, explores a different potential angle to resolving the issue arising at the intersection of AI and copyright law.

Whilst Chapter 7 suggested potential changes to the law, Chapter 9, in summary, argues for changes elsewhere with the law either remaining as-is or only changing slowly and iteratively.

The concepts and arguments made in Chapter 7 could apply to any form of technology. They are not specific to AI, although, e.g., so-called 'deepfakes' are considered at the start of the chapter to illustrate a point (p.179). Here, Lee and Woo argue that the reproductions of material within deepfakes are not simply visible copies of original materials in the same way that traditional copyright infringement might entail, i.e., where verbatim or near-verbatim unauthorised copies of originals are distributed (p.179).

Before presenting their own arguments, Lee and Woo examine a proposition by scholar Jessica Litman that copyright should be recast in law as a right of commercial exploitation (p.179 to 181). This proposition is examined in the context of the changing EU approach to hyperlinks in copyright law along with proposals for reform to copyright law in Hong Kong (p.180). Lee and Woo use this analysis to support the case that copyright law is complex and can have unpredictable outcomes. Rather than proposing reform, however, they argue that this calls for non-statutory controls.

Although the thrust of Lee and Woo's argument is for non-statutory controls, they grant that statutes can satisfactorily be revised iteratively and slowly with care, which—it is reasoned—can be preferable to wholesale reform (p.196).

What type of non-statutory alternative controls do Lee and Woo propose? The main suggestion seems to be that a 'stakeholder-driven educational campaign' may be 'the most reliable way' to protect copyright (p.197). This reviewer has not checked, but it may be the case that Lee and Woo develop and particularise this proposed solution in other works or will do so in the future.

Can Artificial intelligence infringe copyright? Some reflections

Chapter 13 'Can Artificial intelligence infringe copyright? Some reflections', by Enrico Bonadio, Plamen Dinev and Luke McDonagh (from p.245), takes a different approach to Chapters 7 and 9 (summarised above). It considers problems arising in US, EU and UK copyright law with the use of modern AI systems. It is slightly more recently written than the other chapters, as it references the (then state-of-the-art) OpenAI GPT-3 (p. 245).

Bonadio, Dinev and McDonagh consider the use of input data for training deep learning systems (p.246) and note that the need of

AI systems to learn from vast amounts of source material may lead to a risk of copyright infringement (p.247).

The authors consider the doctrine of fair use (p.247), examine the potential of special treatment for AI systems (p.249) and focus on the EU concept of an exemption for transient copies (p.251) as well as the UK exemption for text and data mining (p.252), highlighting that there are significant limits to the exemption when use is in a commercial context.

As well as considering how the law may apply (specifically in the context of training, it seems), Bonadio, Dinev and McDonagh explore how liability may fall for AI infringement, and they consider the allocation of liability where there is no exemption. They explain that this is a difficult and unresolved area (p.253).

Not only are legal challenges considered by the authors, so too are policy challenges (p.255) and although concrete solutions are not offered in this particular chapter, Bonadio, Dinev and McDonagh reach a number of conclusions (p.256 and 257). These include acknowledging that AI systems require extensive volumes of data and outlining that when 'AI-induced infringement' occurs, there is no agreement on any standard framework for allocating liability.

The authors explain that whilst the US has a broad fair-use doctrine that may be applicable to AI systems, the use of such systems in the context of UK and EU law would need to rely on more narrow exemptions such as the EU 'transient copy' principle and the UK 'text and data mining' exemption. These are however narrow and of limited application in practice. The latter, for example, applies to research or cultural heritage institutions.

Bonadio, Dinev and McDonagh conclude that infringement is difficult to govern in the context of AI applications, especially given that computers are not under the jurisdiction of the law, and it can be hard to attribute liability to potential human parties, such as developers, who may not be fully able to appreciate the risks of infringement with AI systems owing to their autonomy – which this reviewer reads in a narrow sense to apply to, e.g., the opaqueness of an AI system's learning process.

Computational trademark infringement and adjudication

Chapter 14 (from p.259) by Daryl Lim is titled 'Computational trademark infringement and adjudication'. This chapter unearths and discusses a number of potentially useful pre-existing datasets as well as prior empirical work in the area, and has particularly insightful analysis of the 'data scarcity' issue affecting legal AI (discussed below).

The chapter itself is organised into five sections (including the introduction and conclusion): Section 2 deals with 'computational consumption' and describes the way that computers have led to changing consumer behaviours which have, to some extent, displaced the need for trademarks. It asks: do we still rely to the same extent on trademarks as a signifier of a product one might prefer when algorithms are curating our purchasing behaviour?; Section 3 deals with computational adjudication, which is self-explanatory though it bears noting that this is in the area of trademark law practice; and Section 4 deals with challenges and responses to computational adjudication – with particular challenges arising from emerging AI techniques.

The two perspectives of this chapter are therefore: how AI systems may change the need for trademarks (and for trademark law), and how AI systems may change the legal practice of trademark law – especially in the realm of adjudication.

This chapter appears to deal with US laws, and it appears (from its footnotes) to have been written between 2020 and 2021. Lim has considered (the now-dominant) GPT technology (e.g., 3.2 / footnote 117) and appears to have adapted the chapter for the book (e.g., reference to Part III in introduction, p.261).

Lim starts by discussing trademark law's 'likelihood of confusion' test, the unique nature of trademark law (trademarks last indefinitely, unlike patents and copyrights) and the patchwork of law that exists at present (in the US). Lim calls for clarity in the law (p.260) and explains how AI can automate legal processes for trademark lawyers. Lim also notes that scholarship on the effects of AI on trademark law is scarce (p.261).

In the chapter, Lim discusses a mix of technologies from meta tags (an aspect of markup languages that stems from the 1990s), recommendation engines used by e-commerce websites (a technology that might be dated to around the 2000s), chess/games engines (from the mid-2010s), and more recent machine learning techniques as well as natural language processing techniques from around the 2020s. (Note, this review includes various rough time estimates by the reviewer for various technologies to show the breadth of technologies covered across the book's chapters. These estimates, often to a rough decade, are not taken from the work.)

Computational consumption

Section 2 (p.261 onwards) on 'computational consumption' reminds us that a trademark serves as a valuable heuristic for busy consumers who have limited time, access of inspection and cognitive capacity to compare products rationally in a saturated marketplace. Lim explains that with the emergence of algorithm-driven e-commerce, the trademark heuristic for consumer choice is becoming less important. Algorithms are, to some extent, replacing the function of trademarks. (p.262) and are increasingly blind to any value in trademarks (p.263). Lim explains that trademarks remain important for online platforms themselves – as the platform's trademark is a starting point for consumers, but once a consumer is within a platform, its algorithms increasingly displace the heuristic of a trademark—to the extent that even infringing products might be offered to consumers (p.264 and 265). Section 2 also considers the ways that US courts have dealt with different factors of digital technology that have encroached on the role traditionally performed by trademarks, including domain names, recommendation engines and website metatags (p.265 and 266)

Computational adjudication

Section 3 (from p.266) discusses the ability of AI technologies to automate certain practices of trademark lawyers and to potentially either resolve disputes or predict judicial outcomes.

Before considering the process of computational adjudication, a key (but thorny) US test is set out – the 'likelihood of confusion' standard. Different approaches to factors that might go towards this are discussed. These range from an eight-point checklist that emerges from case law (p.267) to a simpler two factor test emerging from research (p.268).

The difficulty in dealing with pliable and intuitively understood subjective standards as opposed to objective, binary criminal law-like rules is also discussed, and the suggestion seems to be, from a review of empirical work, that computer systems have historically dealt well with the latter but not the former (p.271). Lim grants that emerging techniques may be changing this (p.272).

Lim highlights that the development of case law over time gives hard edges to subjective standards, e.g., to recite the metaphor used, if a hypothetical subjective motoring law required a 'reasonable speed of driving' rather than a fixed speed then case law might set the cut-off speed as, e.g., 80 mph. Here neural networks are introduced, and the argument is presented that modern AI systems can bring more clarity to the analysis of trademark infringement, given the difficulty of finding hard edges.

Section 3 goes on to discuss execution, i.e., using AI systems in trademark practice and dispute resolution. Some examples are given of existing systems (p.274). Different raw ingredients of technologies are also discussed, including the 'word2vec' approach (developed in recent decades) and 'regular expressions' (a technique developed several decades ago). Lim proposes a trademark recommendation system, drawing on empirical work (which appears to be from around the 2000s) and discussing a range of a range of possible algorithms that a system might use (p.276 – 278). Note, insights might be gained by exposing the datasets from the empirical work reviewed to more modern approaches.

Legal Issues Journal 10(1) 2024: 105-116. ©The UK Law and Society Association

Challenges and responses

Section 4 covers the three issues of bias, accountability and data scarcity.

The subsection on bias (p.279 – 281) discusses algorithmic bias, the nature of statistical prediction and also the nature of human bias. It predicts a potential future where unwanted bias is minimised and ethics teams are involved in system design and use. It highlights that confronting people with the merits of the opposite side's argument statistically reduces the effects of coherence shifts, and that asking lawyers to consider the other side, or reasons why a judge might rule against them, has been empirically shown to mitigate bias (p.281, also p.273).

On accountability (p.281 – 285), the complexity of US trademark law's doctrinal tests is discussed (especially the likelihood of confusion standard) and the utility of AI systems for achieving results that are near-identical to human judgment is contrasted with the difficulty of understanding how an AI system (at least a modern system) reached its results. It is, of course, difficult to properly understand how humans actually achieved their results as well (p.283), but AI systems in particular attract scholarly concerns and public scepticism (p.282). The solution of 'dumbing down' AI systems to use less complex and more accountable techniques is discussed and one solution of using techniques from the early 2000s is discussed which may be promising (albeit that functional capability would likely be reduced). Lim discusses a particular approach called the Monte Carlo Tree Search method (a 2000s computational technique that draws on circa 1940s mathematics). This is presented as a possible compromise for algorithmically assessing the likelihood of confusion standard in a particular case, with fewer issues of bias potentially arising (p.284). Other algorithms are also discussed by Lim (including the nearest neighbour algorithm (p.288)), in very broad terms.

Data scarcity

Here, existing research is discussed which notes the importance of large datasets. Lim highlights that difficulty acquiring these hinders the training of AI for legal tasks (p.285). To explain 'large' in this context, different numbers are given as possible thresholds for the volume of training data needed in different scenarios. Examples are given where different legal AI techniques have needed either millions, tens of thousands, thousands or hundreds of training samples in order to achieve acceptable levels of reliability (p.286 and 267). Clearly, the number of samples depends on the complexity of the task in hand. Similarly, complex tasks may need similarly large datasets (fn 251). Lim considers that training a system to assess against the 'likelihood of confusion' standard might only need a relatively small dataset.

The barrier of data protection law is discussed by Lim here, but only very briefly. Very brief coverage is likely appropriate in the field of trademark law, since the subject matter is the mark. (Here, Lim may have inadvertently highlighted an excellent area of law for testing legal AI systems without raising complex data privacy issues).

Lim concludes with a discussion of AI's ability to assist courts in navigating trademark infringement cases, notes that barriers can be mitigated and calls for AI systems to assist rather than replace the courts.

Conclusion

Overall, this is an excellent research handbook and a reader can expect to be able to 'dip into' chapters repeatedly.

Works of this type inevitably cover both the fields of law and of computer science, and this book is of more use to a practising lawyer or a legal scholar than to a computer scientist. This is since the treatment of the law is relatively focused, necessitating a broad review of a wide mix of relevant technologies. Given the scholarly

Legal Issues Journal 10(1) 2024: 105-116. ©The UK Law and Society Association

nature of the book, it is likely to be of slightly more direct use to legal scholars than to practitioners, although practitioners will find many of the arguments and ideas insightful and any reader is likely to find the book's chapters enjoyable. I am happy to recommend this book.

The reviewer accepted an invitation to review the work and was provided with a review copy. This has not had any impact on the nature of this review. The reviewer is not aware of any other fact that could give rise to any perceived conflict of interests.

Legal Issues Journal

editor@uklsa.co.uk

http://www.legalissuesjournal.com

To advertise with Legal Issues Journal, email editor@uklsa.co.uk

The United Kingdom Law and Society Association

To support the Journal or UKLSA in general,
email president@uklsa.co.uk.

www.uklsa.co.uk